Test Manual

Judith M. Wilkinson and Sharon K. Stoffels

Contemporary Maternal-Newborn Nursing Care

Fifth Edition

Patricia Wieland Ladewig, PhD, RN

Professor and Academic Dean
School for Health Care Professions
Regis University
Denver, Colorado

Marcia L. London, MSN, RNC, NNP

Beth-El College of Nursing and Health Sciences
University of Colorado
Colorado Springs, Colorado

Susan M. Moberly, RNC, ICCE

Labor and Delivery Nurse and Certified Childbirth Educator
Penrose Community Hospital/Centura Health
Colorado Springs, Colorado

Sally B. Olds, MS, RNC, SANE

Professor Emerita
Beth-El College of Nursing and Health Sciences
Colorado Springs, Colorado

Prentice Hall, Upper Saddle River, New Jersey 07458

Notice: Care has been taken to confirm the accuracy of information presented in this book. The authors, editors, and the publisher, however, cannot accept any responsibility for errors or omissions or for consequences from application of the information in this book and make no warranty, express or implied, with respect to its contents.

The authors and publisher have exerted every effort to ensure that drug selections and dosages set forth in this text are in accord with current recommendations and practice at time of publication. However, in view of ongoing research, changes in government regulations, and the constant flow of information relating to drug therapy and drug reactions, the reader is urged to check the package inserts of all drugs for any change in indications of dosage and for added warnings and precautions. This is particularly important when the recommended agent is a new and/or infrequently employed drug.

Pearson Education LTD.
Pearson Education Australia PTY, Limited
Pearson Education Singapore, Pte. Ltd.
Pearson Education North Asia Ltd.
Pearson Education Canada, Ltd.
Pearson Educación de Mexico, S.A. de C.V.
Pearson Education—Japan
Pearson Education Malaysia, Pte. Ltd.

10 9 8 7 6 5 4 3 2
ISBN 0-13-032507-4

This Test Bank to accompany the Fifth Edition of Contemporary Maternal Newborn Nursing Care offers complete coverage of the textbook material and provides an easy-to-use resource from which you can create many unique examinations quickly and efficiently. Questions are numbered by chapter and item number (1.1, 1.2, and so on).

Test items are modeled on the computerized adaptive testing (CAT) NCLEX test plan. Each question is completely freestanding; questions do not refer to previously cited scenarios. Where real-life scenarios are used, they are presented entirely within a single question. For each question, students are to choose the one best answer from the four options. The options do not include "all of the above" or "none of the above."

Test items have been coded with the appropriate category: Cognitive Level, Nursing Process, and Client Needs. These categories are divided in the following ways:

Cognitive Level
Knowledge
Comprehension
Application

Nursing Process
Assessment
Analysis/Diagnosis
Planning
Implementation
Evaluation

Client Needs
The Client Needs category contains subcategories (subjects) that are integrated into the test bank.
Safety = Safe, Effective Care Environment
Management of Care
Safety and Infection Control

Promotion = Health Promotion and Maintenance
Growth and Development Through the Life Span
Prevention and Early Detection of Disease

Psychosocial = Psychosocial Integrity
Coping and Adaptation
Psychosocial Adaptation
Physiological = Physiological Integrity
Basic Care and Comfort
Pharmacological and Parenteral Therapies
Reduction of Risk Potential
Physiological Adaptation

Testing aids are offered free to adopters of the textbook in two forms: the printed test bank and the computerized testing software for Windows 95/98/NT and the Macintosh. With the testing software, you are able to customize test questions and exams. For example, you can choose test items based on Cognitive Level, Nursing Process, and Client Needs classifications. If it is important to you to include test questions specific to your lecture coverage, you may add questions of your own design. If you have any questions about the supplemental material that accompanies Contemporary Maternal-Newborn Nursing Care, Fifth Edition, please contact your Prentice Hall representative.

This Test Bank and the testing software have been developed with you, the instructor, in mind. The authors, editors, and publishers have sought to provide you with a comprehensive testing package that offers quality test items, flexibility, variety, and accuracy. We hope you find it useful.

Additional supplements accompanying Contemporary Maternal Newborn Nursing Care, Fifth Edition for the instructor and the student include:

Student CD-ROM (packaged with each text book)
Instructor's Resource Manual
Instructor's Resouce CD-ROM with Testing Software and PowerPoint Image Collection
Clinical Handbook

Visit our Web site at www.prenhall.com/nursing for additional teaching aids including the Companion Web site, updates, and information on all of our nursing texts.

Contents

Chapter 1
Contemporary Maternal-Newborn Care

a

Comprehension

Assessment

Promotion: Growth and
    Development

1-1. Contemporary childbirth is best characterized by its focus on
      a. family-centered care.
      b. the use of freestanding birthing centers.
      c. outpatient childbirth.
      d. strict infection control measures.

c

Comprehension

Planning

Safety: Management of Care

1-2. The individual ultimately responsible for obtaining an
      informed consent from the client prior to a cesarean section is
      the
      a. admitting nurse.
      b. staff nurse.
      c. physician.
      d. unit manager.

a

Application

Analysis/Diagnosis

Safety: Management of Care

1-3. The ethical issues surrounding abortion and intrauterine fetal
      surgery are similar in that they both
      a. involve maternal-fetal conflict.
      b. involve the newest reproductive technology.
      c. require a court order.
      d. require consent of both parents.

c

Comprehension

Assessment

Safety: Management of Care

1-4. Certified nurse-midwives do which of the following?
      a. Attend home births under the direct supervision of a
      physician.
      b. Give primary care for high-risk clients who are in hospital
      settings.
      c. Give primary care to healthy women during pregnancy and
      birth.
      d. Obtain a physician consultation for any technical
      procedures at delivery.

d

Application

Assessment

Safety: Management of Care

1-5. A 24-year-old Jehovah's Witness has refused to sign a
      consent for blood replacement, even though she is
      hemorrhaging following the birth of her baby. If health care
      providers ignore her wishes and transfuse her, they would be
      violating the ethical principle of
      a. justice.
      b. nonmaleficence.
      c. beneficence.
      d. autonomy.

b

Knowledge

Assessment

Promotion: Growth and
    Development

1-6. Neonatal mortality is defined as the number of deaths of infants less than _____ per 1000 live births.

a. 1 month of age

b. 28 days of age

c. 15 days of age

d. 1 week of age

a

Comprehension

Analysis/Diagnosis

Promotion: Prevention and
    Early Detection

1-7. The maternal death rate in the last 25 years has shown

a. a steady decrease.

b. no significant changes over time.

c. a consistent increase.

d. extreme fluctuations.

b

Knowledge

Assessment

Promotion: Prevention and
    Early Diagnosis

1-8. Which of the following has contributed to the continuing decline of maternal mortality in the United States?

a. The number of home deliveries has significantly increased.

b. Antibiotics are used to prevent and control infection.

c. Recently, the number of physicians specializing in obstetrics has increased.

d. Almost all women in the United States receive prenatal care.

d

Comprehension

Planning

Promotion: Prevention and
    Early Diagnosis

1-9. Maternal-newborn nurses can appropriately use applied statistics

a. only when conducting nursing research.

b. when functioning in the role of counselor or consultant.

c. only under the supervision of an advanced practice nurse.

d. to determine whether a client is a member of a population at risk.

b

Knowledge

Assessment

Promotion: Prevention and
    Early Diagnosis

1-10. The maternal mortality rate includes the number of maternal deaths per

a. 1,000 live births.

b. 100,000 live births.

c. 1,000 pregnancies.

d. 100,000 pregnancies.

b
Application
Planning
Safety: Management of Care

1-11. The maternity nurse's best defense against an accusation of malpractice or negligence is that the nurse

a. followed the physician's written orders.

b. met the American Association of Women's Health, Obstetric and Neonatal Nurses (AWHONN) standards of practice.

c. is a certified nurse midwife or nurse practitioner.

d. was acting on the advice of her nurse manager.

b
Comprehension
Assessment
Promotion: Growth and
    Development

1-12. Which of the following BEST characterizes the activity of the Human Genome Project?

a. cloning

b. genetic mapping

c. genetic manipulation

d. gamete intrafallopian transfer

b
Comprehension
Planning
Safety: Management of Care

1-13. Standards of care, required of all professional nurses, refers to

a. the minimum amount of nursing care required for safe practice.

b. the care that a reasonable, prudent nurse would provide in a particular situation.

c. nursing care as described in policy manuals.

d. the minimum number of professional nurses needed to provide safe care on a unit.

a
Comprehension
Planning
Physiological: Reduction of
    Risk Potential

1-14. Which of the following families might find cord blood banking to be especially useful? A family

a. with a history of leukemia.

b. with a history of infertility.

c. that wishes to select the sex of a future child.

d. that wishes to avoid a future intrauterine fetal surgery.

a
Comprehension
Assessment
Safety: Management of Care

1-15. Which of the following BEST characterizes a "seamless" system of family-centered care?

a. coordination of services

b. reduction of costs

c. quality improvement

d. increased client choice

d
Comprehension
Assessment
Promotion: Prevention and
    Early Detection

1-16. The infant mortality rate in the United States is
a. the highest among the industrialized nations.
b. the lowest among the industrialized nations.
c. rising (more deaths per 1,000).
d. falling (fewer deaths per 1,000).

a
Knowledge
Assessment
Promotion: Growth and
    Development

1-17. The term birth rate refers to the
a. number of live births per 1000 population.
b. the number of live births each year.
c. the average number of births for a given woman.
d. the number of births per 1000 women aged 15 to 44 in a given population.

a
Comprehension
Assessment
Physiological: Physiological
    Adaptation

1-18. The primary reason for performing intrauterine fetal surgery is to
a. correct anatomic lesions that would otherwise be fatal to the fetus.
b. further the research on sex-linked hereditary diseases.
c. reduce risk to the mother by preventing the need for a cesarean birth.
d. treat life-threatening fetal conditions during the third trimester.

b
Knowledge
Planning
Safety: Management of Care

1-19. According to the 1973 Supreme Court decision in *Roe* v. *Wade*, abortion is legal if induced
a. at a federally funded clinic.
b. before the period of viability.
c. to provide tissue for therapeutic research.
d. at a military hospital overseas.

a
Analysis
Assessment
Safety: Management of Care

1-20. A woman in labor has been admitted to the maternity unit with a gunshot wound of the shoulder. When making a decision about the woman's right to privacy and/or confidentiality, the most important principle to consider in this case is
a. protection of the public good.
b. respect for the woman's privacy.
c. professional standards of the American Nurses Association (ANA).
d. requirements of the Joint Commission for Accreditation of Healthcare Organizations (JCAHO).

d
Application
Assessment
Safety: Management of Care

1-21. Which of the following best illustrates an *advanced practice* nursing role?

a. a registered nurse who is the manager of a large obstetrical unit

b. a registered nurse who is the circulating nurse at surgical deliveries (cesarean sections)

c. a clinical nurse specialist working as a staff nurse on a mother-baby unit

d. a clinical nurse specialist whom other nurses consult for her expertise in caring for high-risk infants

c
Comprehension
Assessment
Safety: Management of Care

1-22. Which of the following statements is *TRUE* concerning early discharge following childbirth?

a. Neonates often return to the hospital with respiratory infections.

b. Nurses do not include adequate teaching in their discharge planning.

c. Many women are discharged lacking knowledge and experience in neonatal and self-care.

d. Early discharge often results in postpartum hemorrhage.

a
Knowledge
Assessment
Safety: Management of Care

1-23. Experienced nurses are able to view situations more holistically because they

a. are more aware of subtle cues that indicate client changes.

b. need less supervision in managing complex clinical situations.

c. spend less time giving direct client care.

d. know more about the pathophysiology of diseases.

Chapter 2
Reproductive Anatomy and Physiology

b
Knowledge
Assessment
Promotion: Growth and
    Development

2-1. With intense sexual stimulation, the male penile muscles contract rhythmically, forcefully expelling semen through the urethra. This sudden, forceful expulsion is called
a. erection.
b. ejaculation.
c. intercourse.
d. copulation.

c
Comprehension
Implementation
Promotion: Growth and
    Development

2-2. An adolescent boy asks, "Does the scrotum have a function?" The nurse's best reply is, "The scrotum
a. serves no function that we know of."
b. is a rather insensitive structure that houses the testicles."
c. protects the testes and the sperm."
d. maintains a higher temperature environment than inside the body."

c
Comprehension
Assessment
Promotion: Growth and
    Development

2-3. A man who has had a vasectomy becomes functionally sterile because the sperm
a. are no longer being produced.
b. are no longer motile and fertile.
c. cannot reach the outside of the body.
d. cannot penetrate an ovum.

d
Knowledge
Assessment
Promotion: Growth and
    Development

2-4. The function of the Skene's ducts (paraurethral glands) is to
a. aid in micturition.
b. secrete a spermicidal secretion to aid in birth control.
c. secrete neutral vaginal fluids to aid in fertilization.
d. facilitate sexual intercourse by lubricating the vagina.

c
Knowledge
Assessment
Promotion: Growth and
    Development

2-5. The primary components of the external female reproductive system are the
a. clitoris, vaginal canal, and perineal body.
b. labia, clitoris, and urethra.
c. mons, labia, and clitoris.
d. mons, labia, and vagina.

c
Knowledge
Assessment
Promotion: Growth and
    Development

2-6. The layer of the nonpregnant uterus that undergoes monthly regeneration and renewal is the
a. perimetrium.
b. myometrium.
c. endometrium.
d. corpus.

b
Knowledge
Assessment
Promotion: Growth and
    Development

2-7. The layer of the uterus most involved with the expulsion of the fetus is the
a. perimetrium.
b. myometrium.
c. endometrium.
d. mucosa.

c
Knowledge
Assessment
Promotion: Growth and
    Development

2-8. A portion of postpartum assessment includes visual inspection of the perineal body. This is the area between the
a. mons pubis and the vagina.
b. mons pubis and the anus.
c. vagina and the anus.
d. clitoris and the vagina.

d
Knowledge
Assessment
Promotion: Growth and
    Development

2-9. Which of the following bones moves during labor to provide more room for descent of the fetus? The
a. ilium.
b. ischium.
c. sacrum.
d. coccyx.

a
Comprehension
Assessment
Promotion: Growth and
    Development

2-10. Which of the following correctly describes the mobility of the joints between the innominate bones? They are
a. lined with fibrocartilage, fused, and not moveable.
b. held together by connective tissue and slightly moveable.
c. held together by fibrocartilage and slightly moveable.
d. joined by muscle and ligaments and freely moveable.

a
Knowledge
Assessment
Promotion: Growth and
    Development

2-11. The bony limits of the birth canal are represented by the
a. true pelvis.
b. false pelvis.
c. major pelvis.
d. greater pelvis.

d

Knowledge

Assessment

Promotion: Growth and
    Development

2-12. The diameter of the female pelvis that determines if the fetus can progress downward into the birth canal is the

a. conjugate vera.

b. transverse diameter.

c. diagonal conjugate.

d. obstetric conjugate.

d

Comprehension

Implementation

Promotion: Growth and
    Development

2-13. A pregnant adolescent asks the nurse, "How can a woman's body stretch enough for a baby to come out without tearing?" The nurse's answer should be that the perineal body is able to stretch without tearing during childbirth because of

a. a toned and elastic pubococcygeal muscle.

b. hormonal changes associated with pregnancy.

c. increased blood supply during pregnancy.

d. muscles being mingled with elastic fibers and connective tissue.

b

Comprehension

Analysis/Diagnosis

Promotion: Growth and
    Development

2-14. Which of the following four phases of the menstrual cycle is eliminated if implantation occurs?

a. menstrual phase

b. ischemic phase

c. proliferative phase

d. secretory phase

b

Application

Analysis/Diagnosis

Promotion: Growth and
    Development

2-15. A woman has been unable to complete a full-term pregnancy because the fertilized ovum fails to implant in the uterus. This is most likely due to a lack of which hormone?

a. estrogen

b. progesterone

c. FSH

d. LH

b

Knowledge

Assessment

Promotion: Growth and
    Development

2-16. During which phase of the menstrual cycle does the endometrium thicken?

a. menstrual phase

b. proliferative phase

c. secretory phase

d. ischemic phase

c
Knowledge
Assessment
Promotion: Growth and
    Development

2-17. The vascularity of the uterus increases and the endometrium becomes prepared for a fertilized ovum in which phase of the menstrual cycle?

a. menstrual phase

b. proliferative phase

c. secretory phase

d. ischemic phase

d
Knowledge
Assessment
Promotion: Growth and
    Development

2-18. The corpus luteum begins to degenerate, the estrogen and progesterone levels fall, and the blood supply to the endometrium is reduced in which phase of the menstrual cycle?

a. menstrual phase

b. proliferative phase

c. secretory phase

d. ischemic phase

c
Application
Analysis/Diagnosis
Promotion: Growth and
    Development

2-19. A woman is experiencing *mittelschmerz* and increased vaginal discharge. Her temperature has been increased by 0.6° C (1.0° F) for the past 36 hours. This most likely indicates that

a. menstruation is about to begin.

b. ovulation will occur soon.

c. ovulation has occurred.

d. she is pregnant and will not menstruate.

c
Knowledge
Assessment
Physiological: Basic Care and
    Comfort

2-20. Which of the uterine ligaments contribute to the pain of dysmenorrhea (painful menstruation)?

a. the infudibulopelvic ligaments

b. the broad ligament

c. the uterosacral ligaments

d. the ovarian ligaments

a
Knowledge
Assessment
Promotion: Growth and
    Development

2-21. The hormone that increases contractility of the uterus is

a. estrogen.

b. progesterone.

c. follicle stimulating hormone (FSH).

d. luteinizing hormone (LH).

d
Knowledge
Assessment
Promotion: Growth and
  Development

2-22. The follicle-stimulating hormone (FSH) and luteinizing hormone (LH) are secreted by the
a. hypothalamus.
b. ovaries and testes.
c. posterior pituitary.
d. anterior pituitary.

d
Application
Assessment
Promotion: Growth and
  Development

2-23. During a woman's routine pelvic examination, the clinician can visually examine the
a. body of the uterus.
b. fallopian tubes.
c. ovaries.
d. vaginal introitus.

b
Application
Analysis/Diagnosis
Promotion: Growth and
  Development

2-24. Based on the anatomy of the male external genitalia, which of the following is the most logical cause of inability to achieve erection?
a. weakness or atrophy of the penile muscles
b. poor circulation to the penis
c. an undescended testicle
d. decreased functioning of the seminiferous tubules

c
Knowledge
Assessment
Promotion: Growth and
  Development

2-25. In the male, spermatozoa are produced by the
a. penis.
b. prostate.
c. testes.
d. vas deferens.

a
Knowledge
Assessment
Promotion: Growth and
  Development

2-26. Spermatozoa become motile and fertile during the 2 to 10 days they are stored in the
a. epididymis.
b. vas deferens.
c. prostate gland.
d. urethra.

a
Knowledge
Assessment
Promotion: Growth and
  Development

2-27. During which phase of the menstrual cycle is the endometrium shed?
a. menstrual phase
b. proliferative phase
c. secretory phase
d. ischemic phase

Chapter 3
Conception and Fetal Development

b
Knowledge
Assessment
Promotion: Growth and
    Development

3-1.   In the female, the gametes are produced by the
- a. polar body.
- b. ovaries.
- c. uterus.
- d. fallopian tubes.

b
Knowledge
Assessment
Promotion: Growth and
    Development

3-2.   In order for fertilization to occur, what portion of the sperm must enter the ovum?
- a. the entire sperm
- b. only the head
- c. only the tail
- d. either the head or the tail

a
Knowledge
Assessment
Promotion: Growth and
    Development

3-3.   In females, meiosis *begins* in all oocytes
- a. before birth.
- b. at birth.
- c. during adolescence.
- d. after becoming pregnant.

b
Knowledge
Assessment
Promotion: Growth and
    Development

3-4.   The cell division process that results in two identical cells, each with the same number of chromosomes as the original cell, is called
- a. meiosis.
- b. mitosis.
- c. oogenesis.
- d. gametogenesis.

a
Comprehension
Analysis/Diagnosis
Promotion:Growth and
    Development

3-5.   A client tells you that her mother was a twin, two of her sisters have twins, and several cousins either are twins or gave birth to twins. The client, too, is expecting twins. Because there is a genetic predisposition to twinning in her family, there is a good chance that the client will have
- a. dizygotic twins.
- b. monozygotic twins.
- c. identical twins.
- d. nonzygotic twins.

d
Comprehension
Assessment
Promotion: Growth and
    Development

3-6. When a 46-chromosome cell divides by the process of meiosis, the resulting daughter cells, after the second division, have

    a. 46 double-structured chromosomes.

    b. 46 single chromosomes.

    c. 23 double-structured chromosomes.

    d. 23 single chromosomes.

d
Knowledge
Assessment
Promotion: Growth and
    Development

3-7. Normal variations in characteristics such as hair and eye color are produced by

    a. translocation of chromosomes.

    b. autosomal nondisjunction of chromosomes.

    c. structural mutation of chromatids.

    d. exchange of genetic material between chromatids.

a
Knowledge
Assessment
Promotion: Growth and
    Development

3-8. The chromosomal structure of human beings consists of

    a. 46 chromosomes 22 pairs of autosomes and 1 pair of sex chromosomes.

    b. 42 chromosomes 20 pairs of autosomes and 1 pair of sex chromosomes.

    c. 46 chromosomes 20 pairs of autosomes and 2 pairs of sex chromosomes.

    d. 40 chromosomes 18 pairs of autosomes and 2 pairs of sex chromosomes.

b
Knowledge
Assessment
Promotion: Growth and
    Development

3-9. Where does fertilization of the oocyte usually occur? In the

    a. ovary.

    b. fallopian tube.

    c. upper portion of the uterus.

    d. vagina.

a
Knowledge
Assessment
Promotion: Growth and
    Development

3-10. Once the ovum has entered the fallopian tube, which of the following facilitates movement of the ovum through the tube and toward the uterus?

    a. estrogen-induced tubal peristalsis

    b. progesterone-induced cervical mucus changes

    c. motions of the fallopian fimbriae

    d. movements of the corona radiata of the ovum

b

Application

Analysis/Diagnosis

Promotion: Growth and
    Development

3-11. How are oogenesis and spermatogenesis different from each
other?

a. Oogenesis results in a cell with 23 double-structured
chromosomes.

b. In spermatogenesis, the first meiotic division begins during
puberty.

c. In spermatogenesis, the second meiotic division occurs
during puberty.

d. Oogenesis begins with a 46-chromosome primordial germ
cell (oogonium).

a

Knowledge

Assessment

Promotion: Growth and
    Development

3-12. A teaching plan for presenting information about conception
and fetal development should include the fact that
transportation of the zygote through the fallopian tube and into
the cavity of the uterus takes a minimum of

a. 3 days.

b. 5 days.

c. 12 hours.

d. 18 hours.

a

Knowledge

Assessment

Promotion: Growth and
    Development

3-13. The purpose of the embryonic membranes is to

a. protect and support the embryo.

b. permit symmetric growth of the embryo.

c. provide a means of metabolic and nutrient exchange.

d. help control the temperature of the embryo.

d

Application

Assessment

Promotion: Growth and
    Development

3-14. If only a small volume of sperm is discharged into the vagina,
an insufficient amount of enzymes may be released when they
encounter the ovum. In that case, pregnancy would probably
not result because peristalsis of the fallopian tube would
decrease, making it difficult for the ovum to

a. enter the uterus.

b. the block to polyspermy (cortical reaction) would not occur.

c. the fertilized ovum would be unable to implant in the
uterus.

d. sperm would be unable to penetrate the zona pellucida of
the ovum.

b

Knowledge

Assessment

Promotion: Growth and
    Development

3-15. Where does the zygote begin cellular multiplication? In the

a. ovary.

b. fallopian tube.

c. uterus, before implantation.

d. uterus, after implantation.

a

Application

Analysis/Diagnosis

Promotion: Growth and
Development

3-16. How are the amnion and the chorion similar? They both

a. are embryonic membranes that form at implantation.

b. develop from the blastocyst.

c. develop from the trophoblast.

d. have fingerlike projections called villi.

b

Knowledge

Analysis/Diagnosis

Promotion: Growth and
Development

3-17. What is the correct order in which cellular multiplication occurs after a sperm enters an ovum?

a. zygote, trophoblast, morula

b. zygote, morula, trophoblast

c. morula, trophoblast, zygote

d. morula, zygote, trophoblast

c

Knowledge

Assessment

Promotion: Growth and
Development

3-18. When does true placental formation begin? During

a. conception.

b. implantation.

c. the third week of gestation.

d. the third month of gestation.

b

Comprehension

Analysis/Diagnosis

Promotion: Growth and
Development

3-19. Which of the following may cause hydramnios?

a. The fetus swallows too much amniotic fluid.

b. The fetus does not swallow enough amniotic fluid.

c. There is obstruction of fetal urine outflow.

d. There is keratinization of the fetal skin.

a

Knowledge

Assessment

Promotion: Growth and
Development

3-20. The placenta is divided into segments called

a. cotyledons.

b. decidua.

c. syncytium.

d. villi.

c

Comprehension

Implementation

Promotion: Growth and
Development

3-21. When presenting information about fetal development to a group of high school girls, one of the girls asks the nurse to explain the functions of the amniotic fluid. The nurse's response should be, "The amniotic fluid cushions the embryo/fetus against mechanical injury, controls the embryo's temperature, and

a. provides a means of nutrient exchange for the embryo/fetus."

b. creates adherence of the amnion."

c. allows freedom of movement so the embryo/fetus can change position."

d. provides for fetal respiration and metabolism."

c
Knowledge
Assessment
Promotion: Growth and
    Development

a
Knowledge
Assessment
Promotion: Growth and
    Development

b
Comprehension
Assessment
Promotion: Growth and
    Development

a
Comprehension
Implementation
Promotion: Growth and
    Development

b
Application
Analysis/Diagnosis
Promotion: Growth and
    Development

3-22. After 20 weeks' gestation, the volume of amniotic fluid is
    a. 100 to 300 mL.
    b. 350 to 650 mL.
    c. 700 to 1000 mL.
    d. 1000 to 1500 mL.

3-23. When assessing a placenta and umbilical cord at delivery, the nurse must know that the normal cord has
    a. 1 vein and 2 arteries.
    b. 2 veins and 1 artery.
    c. 1 vein and 1 artery.
    d. 2 veins and 2 arteries.

3-24. Which of the following would be typical of a fetus at 20 weeks?
    a. The fetus has a body weight of 780 g.
    b. The fetus actively sucks and swallows amniotic fluid.
    c. Formation of urine begins.
    d. Lanugo is disappearing.

3-25. At her first prenatal visit a woman and the nurse are discussing fetal development. The client asks, "When will my baby actually have a heart?" The nurse should reply, "The heart of an embryo is a distinguishable organ by the _____ week of development."
    a. 8th
    b. 14th
    c. 17th
    d. 24th

3-26. A woman is 7 months pregnant and has come to the obstetrical clinic for a routine prenatal examination. During the assessment, the nurse hears a soft blowing sound above the mother's symphysis pubis. The rate of sound is synchronous with the mother's heartbeat. The nurse identifies this as
    a. a normal sound called funic souffle.
    b. a normal sound called uterine souffle.
    c. an abnormal sound representing an aortic aneurysm.
    d. an abnormal sound representing a false knot in the cord.

d

Comprehension

Assessment

Promotion: Growth and
Development

3-27. The placenta produces hormones that are vital to the function of the fetus. Which hormone is primarily responsible for the maintenance of pregnancy past the 11th week?

a. human chorionic gonadotropin (hCG)

b. human placental lactogen (hPL)

c. estrogen

d. progesterone

c

Knowledge

Assessment

Promotion: Growth and
Development

3-28. The post-conception age of the newborn is usually

a. 32-34 weeks.

b. 35-37 weeks.

c. 38-40 weeks.

d. 42-44 weeks.

b

Comprehension

Assessment

Promotion: Growth and
Development

3-29. The embryo's arm and leg buds are well developed and the brain is differentiated by the _____ week.

a. 3rd

b. 4th to 5th

c. 6th

d. 9th to 12th

b

Knowledge

Assessment

Promotion: Growth and
Development

3-30. During the _____ week, the brain is developing rapidly and the nervous system is complete enough to provide some regulation of body function.

a. 17th to 20th

b. 25th to 28th

c. 29th to 32nd

d. 33rd to 36th

a

Knowledge

Assessment

Promotion: Growth and
Development

3-31. At the end of the _____ week, the embryo is sufficiently developed to be called a fetus.

a. 8th

b. 12th

c. 18th

d. 22nd

b

Knowledge

Assessment

Promotion: Growth and
Development

3-32. The fragile blood vessels of the umbilical cord are not compressed by the pressure of the uterus because the vessels are protected by

a. a cushion of amniotic fluid.

b. a padding of Wharton's jelly.

c. a thick muscle layer.

d. highly absorbent vessel walls.

3-33. Because the fetus metabolizes glucose rapidly, it must be transported rapidly from maternal blood (where it is in a higher concentration) to the fetal blood. By what placental mechanism does this occur?

a. simple diffusion

b. pinocytosis

c. facilitated and active transport

d. simple diffusion and bulk flow

3-34. A pregnant woman tells the midwife, "I've heard that if I eat certain foods during my pregnancy, the baby will be a boy." The nurse's response should explain that this is a myth and that the sex of the baby is determined at the time of

a. ejaculation.

b. fertilization.

c. implantation.

d. differentiation.

3-35. During a prenatal examination, a client asks, "How does my baby get air?" The nurse would give correct information by saying,

a. "The lungs of the fetus carry out respiratory gas exchange in utero."

b. "The placenta assumes the function of the fetal lungs by supplying oxygen and allowing the excretion of carbon dioxide into your bloodstream."

c. "The blood from the placenta is carried through the umbilical artery, which penetrates the abdominal wall of the fetus."

d. "The fetus is able to obtain sufficient oxygen due to the fact that your hemoglobin concentration is 50 percent greater during pregnancy."

3-36. Which of the following contains undifferentiated cells? The

a. blastocyst

b. ectoderm

c. mesoderm

d. endoderm

a

Knowledge

Assessment

Promotion: Growth and
Development

3-37. The male's haploid number of chromosomes are carried in which part of the spermatozoon?

a. head

b. middle piece

c. mitochondria

d. flagellum

c

Knowledge

Assessment

Promotion: Growth and
Development

3-38. The blastocyst implants itself in the uterine lining approximately _____ day(s) after fertilization.

a. 1 to 2

b. 3 to 5

c. 7 to 10

d. 12 to 14

a

Comprehension

Planning

Promotion: Growth and
Development

3-39. A couple wishes to conceive. They can improve their chances if they have intercourse within _____ hours after the woman ovulates.

a. 12-24

b. 21-36

c. 7-48

d. 49-72

a

Comprehension

Assessment

Promotion: Growth and
Development

3-40. In the _____ week, the embryo is approximately 2.5 - 3 cm long, the external genitals are visible, and long bones are beginning to form.

a. 8th

b. 16th

c. 24th

d. 28th

Chapter 4
Women's Health Care

c
Comprehension
Assessment
Physiological:
Reduction of Risk Potential

4-1. A 19-year-old woman comes to the gynecologist's office. When the nurse asks the reason for visit, the woman explains that she has never had a menstrual period, and that she is concerned there may be something wrong. The diagnosis that most accurately describes the client's condition is

a. primary dysmenorrhea.

b. secondary infertility.

c. primary amenorrhea.

d. secondary amenorrhea.

b
Knowledge
Assessment
Physiological: Reduction of
    Risk Potential

4-2. A client is complaining of having heavier than normal bleeding during her menstrual period. Her nurse correctly documents this subjective information in the chart as

a. metorrhagia.

b. menorrhagia.

c. polymenorrhea.

d. hypermenorrhea.

c
Application
Implementation
Physiological: Basic Care and
    Comfort

4-3. A client asks her nurse, "Is it okay for me to take a tub bath during the heavy part of my menstruation?" The correct response by the nurse is,

a. "Tub baths are contraindicated during menstruation."

b. "You should shower and douche daily instead."

c. "Either a bath or shower is fine at this time."

d. "You should bathe and use a feminine deodorant spray during menstruation."

c
Comprehension
Planning
Promotion: Prevention and
    Early Detection

4-4. What should the nurse tell a client about using tampons during heavy menstrual flow?

a. Tampons should be avoided when the menstrual flow is heavy.

b. Super tampons with added deodorants are recommended for the day, while regular tampons may be worn at night.

c. Tampons should be used during the day; change to napkins at night when flow is lighter.

d. Tampons are recommended for use at the end of the menstrual period rather than at the beginning.

c

Knowledge

Assessment

Physiological: Reduction of
    Risk Potential

4-5. A 32-year-old woman has a medical diagnosis of premenstrual syndrome (PMS). Compared to other women with this diagnosis, her age is

a. lower.

b. higher.

c. typical.

d. irrelevant.

a

Application

Planning

Physiological: Physiological
    Adaptations

4-6. A teaching plan for a client with premenstrual syndrome (PMS) should include a recommendation to restrict her intake of

a. coffee, tea, colas, and chocolate cake.

b. high-starch foods such as potatoes and spaghetti.

c. chicken, eggs, and fish.

d. breads, cereals, and beans.

a

Comprehension

Planning

Physiological: Physiological
    Adaptation

4-7. Which vitamins seem to be most helpful in reducing the symptoms of PMS?

a. B6 and E.

b. C and E.

c. A and C.

d. A and D.

c

Comprehension

Implementation

Physiological: Physiological
    Adaptation

4-8. Which of the following recommendations would be helpful to a client in reducing her symptoms of PMS? The woman should

a. take estrogen supplements.

b. avoid strenuous physical activity.

c. enroll in a program of aerobic exercises.

d. reduce salt intake and oral fluids.

d

Knowledge

Assessnent

Physiological: Reduction of
    Risk Potential

4-9. The physiological factor that is thought to be responsible for dysmenorrhea is an increase in the production of

a. estrogen.

b. progesterone.

c. oxytocin.

d. prostaglandin.

a
Application
Implementation
Promotion: Growth and
    Development

4-10. A 47-year-old woman is complaining of "hot flashes" associated with menopause. She states that she fears something is going wrong inside her body because her sexual drives have increased recently. The nurse's BEST response would be

a. "This is not unusual. Many women report that they have an increased interest in sex during menopause."

b. "Most women report a decreased interest in sex during menopause; however, there is nothing wrong with your increased interest."

c. "Interest in sex is an individual desire; it is not associated with menopause."

d. "Women who were sexually active prior to menopause usually remain sexually active during and after menopause."

b
Application
Implementation
Physiological: Basic Care and
    Comfort

4-11. A menopausal woman tells her nurse that she experiences discomfort from vaginal dryness during sexual intercourse and asks, "What should I use as a lubricant?" The nurse should recommend

a. petroleum jelly.

b. a water-soluble lubricant.

c. body cream or body lotion.

d. less frequent intercourse.

b
Knowledge
Assessment
Physiological: Reduction of
    Risk Potential

4-12. The major reason the vulvular organs atrophy as a woman ages is that there is a decrease in

a. blood supply.

b. hormonal activity.

c. nerve impulses.

d. sexual activity.

b
Application
Assessment
Promotion: Growth and
    Development

4-13. An RN is working in an OB-Gyn clinic. When taking a sexual history from a client, the nurse should

a. ask questions that the client can answer with a "yes" or "no."

b. ask mostly open-ended questions.

c. write down everything the client says during the interview.

d. try not to make much direct contact.

a

Application

Assessment

Promotion: Growth and Development

b

Comprehension

Analysis

Psychological: Growth and Development

c

Comprehension

Analysis/Diagnosis

Promotion: Prevention and Early Detection

d

Application

Analysis/Diagnosis

Promotion: Prevention and Early Detection

4-14. A complete history includes information about any history of sexually transmitted diseases. The best way for a nurse to handle this subject is to

a. make a general statement, then proceed to a more direct question.

b. ask direct questions to obtain the information she needs.

c. apologize for having to ask such personal questions.

d. begin the interview with questions that may be embarrassing.

4-15. A nurse's responsibilities include counseling clients concerning sexuality. In order for her to be effective in this role, it is *most* important that she

a. have a great deal of knowledge about the client and her needs.

b. be aware of her own feelings, values, and attitudes about sex.

c. be aware of her client's feelings, values, and attitudes about sex.

d. complete an in-depth study of sexual functions and behaviors.

4-16. A client asks, "Can you explain to us how to use the basal body temperature method to detect ovulation and prevent pregnancy?" The correct reply would be

a. "Take your temperature every evening at the same time and keep a record for a period of several weeks. A noticeable drop in temperature indicates that ovulation has occurred."

b. "Take your temperature every day at the same time and keep a record of the findings. A noticeable rise in temperature indicates ovulation."

c. "Take your temperature each day, immediately upon awakening, and keep a record of each finding. A noticeable drop in temperature indicates that ovulation is about to occur."

d. "This is an unscientific and unproved method of determining ovulation and is not recognized as a means of birth control."

4-17. A couple wants the most "natural" contraceptive method possible; they do not want to use any devices or substances. Which method should the nurse recommend?

a. intrauterine device (IUD)

b. symptothermal

c. basal body temperature

d. calendar (rhythm)

a

Application

Analysis/Diagnosis

Promotion: Prevention and
　　Early Detection

4-18. How is the cervical mucus method of contraception *different from* the calendar (rhythm) method? The cervical mucus method

a. is more effective for women with irregular cycles.

b. is free, safe, and acceptable to women of many religions.

c. provides an increased awareness of the body.

d. requires no artificial substances or devices.

c

Application

Planning

Promotion: Prevention and
　　Early Detection

4-19. Instructions concerning the use of a diaphragm should include that it is an excellent method of contraception provided the woman

a. does not use any creams or jellies with it.

b. removes it promptly following intercourse and then douches.

c. leaves it in place for 6 hours following intercourse.

d. inserts it at least 2 hours prior to intercourse.

c

Comprehension

Planning

Promotion:
　　Prevention and Early
　　Detection

4-20. Instructions concerning the use of a condom should include that it is an excellent method of contraception provided the condom is

a. applied immediately before ejaculation.

b. applied tightly over the end of the penis.

c. held and withdrawn properly after ejaculation.

d. withdrawn after the penis becomes flaccid.

a

Comprehension

Analysis

Promotion: Prevention and
　　Early Detection

4-21. A client asks the nurse about the effectiveness of "the pill" as a method of contraception. The nurse should explain to the client that oral contraceptives

a. are a very reliable method of contraception but may produce undesirable side effects.

b. are only reliable as a method of contraception after taken for at least 3 months.

c. have undesirable side effects that pose too great a risk for most women.

d. provide good contraception and are safer than all other methods except fertility awareness.

d
Application
Implementation
Promotion: Prevention and
    Early Detection

4-22. Which mechanical method of contraception should the nurse suggest to a woman who says, "I want to be able to make love spontaneously when the mood hits me; and I don't want anything to change the sensations"?

a. condom

b. diaphragm

c. female condom

d. intrauterine device (IUD)

d
Knowledge
Planning
Promotion: Prevention and
    Early Detection

4-23. One advantage of the female condom is that it

a. is less expensive than other methods of birth control.

b. is economical because it can be used more than once.

c. contains spermicide to add to its effectiveness in preventing pregnancy.

d. provides some protection against sexually transmitted diseases.

b
Knowledge
Planning
Physiological:
    Pharmacological and
    Parenteral

4-24. A woman is starting to use oral contraceptives. She should be advised to contact her health care provider if she experiences

a. breast tenderness.

b. severe headaches.

c. swelling of the ankles.

d. increased appetite.

d
Comprehension
Planning
Physiological: Reduction of
    Risk Potential

4-25. A woman has just been fitted with an IUD (intrauterine device). She will have a follow-up examination in six weeks. Meanwhile, she should contact her health care provider if she has

a. intermittent uterine cramping.

b. irregular menses.

c. intermittent bleeding.

d. chills or fever.

b
Comprehension
Planning
Physiological:
    Pharmacological and
    Parenteral

4-26. A 28-year-old woman has PMS (premenstrual syndrome). She is complaining of frequent headaches, irritability, depression, and breast tenderness associated with her menstrual periods. She will probably be treated with which hormone?

a. estrogen

b. progesterone

c. prostaglandins

d. testosterone

d

Application

Assessment

Physiological: Reduction of
  Risk Potential

4-27. Which of the following women is at highest risk for secondary dysmenorrhea? One who

a. has never been pregnant.

b. has never had intercourse.

c. takes oral contraceptives.

d. uses an intrauterine device (IUD).

a

Application

Planning

Physiological: Basic Care and
  Comfort

4-28. To relieve discomfort from dysmenorrhea, you should advise a client to

a. apply heat to her abdomen and back and drink hot liquids.

b. keep her activities to a minimum during menstruation.

c. take an analgesic every 4 hours and use ice packs on her back.

d. seriously consider having a hysterectomy.

b

Application

Implementation

Promotion: Prevention and
  Early Detection

4-29. A woman says, "My mother told me that I should douche to keep from getting pregnant." The nurse should tell her that douching, as a means of contraception, is

a. effective only if used in conjunction with a diaphragm.

b. not at all effective and may in fact facilitate conception.

c. usually reliable, but must be done immediately after intercourse to be effective.

d. dependent upon the type, temperature, and amount of solution used.

a

Application

Planning

Promotion: Prevention and
  Early Detection

4-30. A woman has made an appointment to have a Pap (Papanicolaou) smear. The nurse should tell her that before coming in for this test, the woman should

a. not douche or have intercourse for 24 hours.

b. not bathe or shower before coming in.

c. bathe and douche regardless of whether she has intercourse.

d. bathe and douche only if she has intercourse.

c

Comprehension

Analysis/Diagnosis

Promotion: Growth and
  Development

4-31. Which of the following women is at high risk for cervical cancer? One who

a. became sexually active after age 30.

b. has never been pregnant.

c. has had several different sex partners.

d. uses tampons instead of vaginal pads.

a

Comprehension

Analysis/Diagnosis

Promotion: Prevention and
  Early Detection

4-32. In determining whether to *begin* mammography screening for
a woman, the most important risk factor to consider is

a. her present age.

b. whether her breasts are sensitive.

c. age at onset of her menses.

d. whether she has had children.

b

Comprehension

Implementation

Promotion: Prevention and
  Early Detection

4-33. To confirm the diagnosis of fibrocystic breast disease, a
physician has ordered a mammogram. The client asks, "What
is a mammogram?" The nurse's correct reply would be, "A
mammogram is

a. soft tissue radiography which visualizes breast tissue by the
use of contrast media."

b. a non-painful, non-invasive, soft-tissue radiograph of the
breast."

c. a method of visualizing the soft tissue of the breast by using
high doses of radiation."

d. a radiograph specific to the visualization of malignant
tumors of the breast."

d

Comprehension

Planning

Physiological: Reduction of
  Risk Potential

4-34. In addition to the pain, one of the reasons many women with
endometriosis seek medical care is due to resultant

a. amenorrhea.

b. anovulatory cycles.

c. increased vaginal discharge.

d. infertility.

a

Application

Planning

Physiological: Physiological
  Adaptation

4-35. A woman was admitted with a diagnosis of toxic shock
syndrome. She is being discharged from the hospital today.
The nurse's discharge instructions should include telling the
woman to

a. use sanitary napkins and avoid the use of tampons.

b. use a diaphragm instead of a coil as a means of birth
control.

c. limit sexual intercourse to only 1 or 2 safe partners.

d. have her sexual partner wear a condom until she is no
longer toxic.

b

Comprehension

Analysis/Diagnosis

Physiological: Reduction of
  Risk Potential

4-36. Which of the following women is predisposed to
vulvovaginal candidiasis (monilial vaginitis)? One who

a. uses vaginal lubricants.

b. is taking oral antibiotics.

c. takes large doses of vitamins.

d. uses a diaphragm for contraception.

a

Application

Planning

Physiological:
  Pharmacological and
  Parenteral

4-37. The physician has prescribed metronidazole (Flagyl) for a woman diagnosed with trichomoniasis. The nurse's instructions to the woman should be,

a. "Both partners must be treated with the medication."

b. "Alcohol should be limited while taking this medication."

c. "It will turn your urine orange."

d. "It may produce drowsiness."

b

Knowledge

Assessment

Physiological: Physiological
  Adaptation

4-38. Trichomoniasis is a sexually transmitted disease caused by a

a. virus.

b. protozoan.

c. bacterium.

d. spirochete.

c

Comprehension

Assessment

Physiological: Reduction of
  Risk Potential

4-39. A woman has been admitted to the hospital with pelvic inflammatory disease (PID). The nurse will observe her carefully because she knows that women with PID are at risk for developing

a. appendicitis.

b. cholecystitis.

c. salpingitis.

d. vulvitis.

b

Comprehension

Assessment

Promotion: Prevention and
  Early Detection

4-40. Which of the following women is at increased risk for a urinary tract infection? One who

a. is not sexually active.

b. suppresses the desire to urinate.

c. has never been pregnant.

d. is in a high-income socioeconomic group.

c

Comprehension

Assessment

Physiological: Reduction of
  Risk Potential

4-41. Venereal warts should be treated because of their possible link to

a. infertility.

b. pyelonephritis.

c. cervical cancer.

d. vaginal cancer.

d

Knowledge

Assessment

Promotion: Growth and
  Development

4-42. Failure of coitus interruptus as a method of birth control usually occurs because of lack of

a. knowledge.

b. experience.

c. aptitude.

d. self-control.

a

Application

Analysis/Diagnosis

Promotion: Prevention and
   Early Detection

4-43. Which of the following is MOST important when screening a woman for partner abuse?

a. ensuring privacy and confidentiality

b. conveying warmth and empathy

c. asking specific, direct questions about abuse

d. clarifying her myths about battering

a

Application

Analysis/Diagnosis

Psychosocial: Psychosocial
   Adaptation

4-44. A woman has come to the emergency room with multiple bruises over her body and a small laceration over her upper lip. She says she fell down the stairs while doing her housework. Which of the following observations would MOST likely cause you to suspect that she has been a victim of battering? The client

a. is hesitant in providing details about how the injuries occurred.

b. was accompanied to the ER by her mother instead of her partner.

c. seems eager to go back home.

d. does not seem to be in pain.

d

Application

Implementation

Psychosocial: Psychosocial
   Adaptation

4-45. A woman has been living in a shelter to escape from an abusive partner. However, she has decided to return home and insists that her mind is made up. What action should the nurse take?

a. Get a restraining order from the court to protect her from her husband.

b. Do not let her leave. Tell her that if she goes back now, her husband will probably kill her.

c. Call the police and ask them to accompany her home

d. Help her make a detailed plan for escaping again, and give her emergency telephone numbers to call.

c

Application

Implementation

Promotion: Prevention and
   Early Detection

4-46. During the initial interview, the RN discovers that the client, age 30, does not perform regular breast self-examinations (BSE). In addition to teaching her the proper technique of BSE, the nurse should also advise her that "BSE should be performed once a month

a. just prior to the beginning of your menstrual period."

b. at the end of your menstrual period."

c. about one week after your menstrual period."

d. immediately following ovulation."

a

Knowledge

Planning

Promotion: Prevention and
    Early Detection

4-47. Other than abstinence, which of the following contraceptive methods provides the BEST protection against sexually transmitted infections?

    a. condom

    b. diaphragm

    c. spermicides

    d. cervical cap

c

Comprehension

Application

Physiological: Reduction of
    risk potential

4-48. How are gonorrhea and herpes genitalis similar? Both

    a. require treatment of all sexual partners in order to cure the disease.

    b. are asymptomatic in the majority of women.

    c. are a danger to a newborn born through the infected birth canal.

    d. include pain and flu-like symptoms in the primary episode.

c

Comprehension

Planning

Physiological: Reduction of
    Risk Potential

4-49. A 27-year-old woman has been experiencing severe pelvic pain and dyspareunia. Her gynecologist performed a laparoscopy and diagnosed endometriosis. Since she has indicated she would like to get pregnant, the expected treatment of her endometriosis would include

    a. prostaglandins.

    b. antibiotics.

    c. danazol.

    d. estrogen.

4-50. A 35-year-old waitress has been diagnosed by her gynecologist as having bilateral fibrocystic breast disease. When assessing the woman's breasts, the nurse finds palpable nodules that are similar in both breasts. The client asks, "Can you tell by feeling if these nodules are cancerous?" The nurse's best reply would be

a. "Cysts are usually well-circumscribed, tender, and movable, and there would be no retraction of the surrounding tissue. A malignancy of this size would probably not be tender or movable, and often there is retraction of the skin in the surrounding tissue."

b. "Cysts are irregular in shape and are not usually movable. When there is a malignancy, the mass has well-defined margins and is movable."

c. "With fibrocystic disease such as yours, there is pain, the cysts are large, solid, irregular masses, and there is usually a discharge from the nipple. These signs are not present when there is a malignancy."

d. "It is impossible to distinguish a benign tumor from a malignant tumor by a physical evaluation. They feel basically the same."

4-51. A client asks the nurse if he will be sterile immediately following a vasectomy. The correct answer would be

a. "You may still ejaculate live sperm for 4 to 6 months following a vasectomy."

b. "You may ejaculate live sperm for 3 to 4 days following a vasectomy."

c. "It takes 1 to 2 months and up to 36 ejaculations to clear the live sperm."

d. "A successful vasectomy provides immediate sterilization."

4-52. A couple has come to the Health Department to discuss various methods of birth control with the family planning nurse. They ask, "What kind of birth control do you think we should use?" The nurse's best reply initially would be

a. "The most effective method of fertility control is the birth control pill."

b. "The various forms of mechanical contraceptives are the most reliable methods of birth control."

c. "The intrauterine device (IUD) is relatively problem-free and provides the best success rate for fertility control."

d. "A birth control method must meet your individual needs."

d

Application

Implementation

Physiological: Reduction of
    Risk Potential

4-53. A client with fibrocystic disease asks her nurse, "Is it necessary for me to perform regular breast self-examinations? My breasts are so lumpy I can't be sure what I'm feeling. I would rather come and let you check my breasts periodically." The nurse should reply,

a. "You will not need to do regular breast self-examinations (BSE) as long as you are faithful about coming to the office on a routine basis."

b. "With fibrocystic disease, breast changes occur frequently. You should do BSE at least once a week to detect changes."

c. "I will be glad to come to your home and examine your breasts on a routine basis."

d. "It is important for you to perform periodic BSE. You know how your breasts feel, and you can detect any changes."

a

Knowledge

Assessment

Physiological: Prevention and
    Early Detection

4-54. The *first* symptom of cystitis is usually

a. pain when urinating.

b. blood in the urine.

c. inability to void.

d. high fever (102°F or more).

a

Knowledge

Assessment

Promotion: Growth and
    Development

4-55. Which of the following medical terms means the beginning of menstruation?

a. menarche

b. climacteric

c. amenorrhea

d. gynecomastia

d

Application

Planning

Psychosocial: Psychosocial
    Adaptation

4-56. A 35-year-old client in the women's health clinic has just told the nurse about being abused by her husband for the past 10 years. The nurse's MOST appropriate intervention, *initially*, is to

a. offer to call the police and help her to file charges.

b. ask her to tell you the details surrounding the abuse.

c. reassure her that many women experience the same problem.

d. listen to her account of the situation and offer support.

b
Comprehension
Assessment
Psychosocial: Coping and
    Adaptation

4-57. A client in the women's health clinic has just told the nurse about being abused by her husband for the past 10 years. When working with the client, which of the following emotional responses should the nurse expect her to demonstrate?

a. avoidance of the issue

b. ambivalence toward her husband

c. associative looseness

d. profound apathy

Chapter 5
Families with Special Reproductive Concerns

c

Application

Implementation

Physiological:
    Pharmacological and
    Parenteral

5-1. A woman is being treated for infertility with Clomid (clomiphene citrate). A few days after starting this medication, she calls the clinic and tells you that she is having some blurred vision and hot flashes. You should tell her

a. that you will have the physician call her before the end of the day.

b. that she should come to the clinic right away to be seen by a physician.

c. to avoid bright lights, increase her fluid intake, and use fans to help her feel cooler.

d. to stop taking the medication for a day or two to see if these side effects disappear.

b

Comprehension

Evaluation

Physiological:
    Pharmacological and
    Parenteral

5-2. A woman has just finished a five-day course of Clomid (clomiphene citrate). If she does not have a period this month,

a. it means that she is definitely pregnant.

b. she should be checked for pregnancy before starting another trial of Clomid.

c. the physician will prescribe a longer trial of Clomid, to begin as soon as she is late for her period.

d. it means that if she is pregnant, she must have a therapeutic abortion.

c

Application

Implementation

Physiological: Reduction of
    Risk Potential

5-3. A client is to have a hysterosalpingogram. She asks you, "Is it painful?" Your best reply would be,

a. "There is no pain associated with the hysterosalpingogram."

b. "You will be asleep for the procedure and will feel nothing at all."

c. "You may have some pain in your shoulder, especially when you sit up."

d. "You may have some pain in your abdomen and in around your diaphragm, but you should not experience severe pain."

a

Application

Planning

Physiological: Reduction of
    Risk Potential

5-4. When a couple asks what a postcoital examination is for, the nurse's best reply would be, "The purpose of this test is to determine the

a. ability of the sperm to survive the cervical barrier."

b. quantity of viable sperm that are ejaculated."

c. quality of viable sperm that are ejaculated."

d. presence of an alkaline or acidic environment."

a

Comprehension

Analysis/Diagnosis

Physiological: Reduction of
    Risk Potential

5-5. A couple has been trying for 2 years to have a baby, but they have been unable to conceive. The woman has never been pregnant. The term that describes their situation is

a. primary infertility.

b. secondary infertility.

c. psychological infertility.

d. physiological infertility.

c

Knowledge

Evaluation

Physiological: Reduction of
    Risk Potential

5-6. Which of the following is a possible side effect of hysterosalpingography?

a. decreased patency of the fallopian tubes

b. intraperitoneal hemorrhage.

c. pelvic inflammatory disease.

d. distortions of the uterine cavity.

d

Application

Analysis/Diagnosis

Promotion: Prevention and
    Early Detection

5-7. What do tests for levels of progesterone, thyroid stimulating hormone, and androgen have in common? They

a. are performed using a sample of maternal urine.

b. provide information about endometrial receptivity.

c. provide information about uterine blood flow.

d. are used to evaluate ovulatory function.

b

Application

Analysis/Diagnosis

Promotion: Prevention and
    Early Detection

5-8. Evaluation of a woman's cervical mucus reveals that it is thin, watery, and profuse. It can be stretched to 6 cm, and ferning is observed when it is air dried on a glass slide. How would you interpret this information? The woman is

a. at or near ovulation; all findings are normal.

b. at or near ovulation; all findings are normal except that the elasticity is slightly less than desired.

c. at least 24 hours postovulation; all findings are normal.

d. at least 24 hours postovulation; all findings are normal, except that ferning should not be present.

c

Application

Analysis/Diagnosis

Physiological: Reduction of
    Risk Potential

5-9. How are a hysteroscopy and a laparoscopy alike? They both

a. are performed under general anesthesia.

b. require a puncture through the umbilical area.

c. use a fiberoptic instrument for visualization.

d. allow for direct visualization of the uterus, tubes, and pelvic organs.

c
Comprehension
Planning
Promotion: Prevention and
    Early Detection

5-10. To maximize their potential for fertilization, a couple should engage in intercourse, beginning 3-4 days prior to and continuing for 2-3 days after the expected time of ovulation. The preferred frequency is

a. twice a day.

b. every day.

c. every other day.

d. once a week.

b
Comprehension
Analysis/Diagnosis
Psychosocial: Coping and
    Adaptation

5-11. For infertile couples, the most difficult aspect of their problem is likely to be the

a. financial burden.

b. emotional aspect.

c. painful and time-consuming testing.

d. decision to adopt or remain childless.

b
Knowledge
Assessment
Promotion: Growth and
    Development

5-12. At what age does the risk for chromosomal abnormalities first become a concern for the childbearing woman (i.e., greater than a 1/200 risk)?

a. 30 years

b. 35 years

c. 40 years

d. 45 years

d
Application
Planning
Promotion: Prevention and
    Early Detection

5-13. A 39-year-old woman is pregnant. Because of her age, an amniocentesis was performed during the 16th week of gestation. Just before the procedure, the client asked her nurse to explain why it was being done. The nurse should explain that the test is performed to

a. ensure the birth of a normal child.

b. detect genetic abnormalities so that an abortion can be done.

c. begin early treatment of an affected fetus.

d. detect any abnormalities of the fetus.

a
Application
Planning
Promotion: Prevention and
    Early Detection

5-14. A pregnant woman is to have a screening test for neural tube defects. She should be told

a. "You will need to go to the lab to have some blood drawn."

b. "We will need to schedule an amniocentesis for you next week."

c. "Save your urine in this container for 24 hours, then bring it back to the lab the same day."

d. "Please give us a clean-catch urine specimen before you leave today."

d
Comprehension
Analysis/Diagnosis
Safety: Management of Care

5-15. Which of the following families who wish to have a child should the nurse refer to a genetic counselor? One in which the woman

a. has a history of sexually transmitted diseases and pelvic inflammatory disease.

b. has a partner who is HIV positive.

c. is 25 years old and has been unable to conceive after a year of unprotected intercourse.

d. is pregnant and will be 40 years old at the time of birth.

b
Knowledge
Assessment
Promotion: Growth and
 Development

5-16. A normal female karyotype consists of

a. 44 autosomes and two Y sex chromosomes.

b. 44 autosomes and two X sex chromosomes.

c. 44 autosomes plus one X and one Y sex chromosome.

d. 46 autosomes plus one X and one Y sex chromosome.

c
Application
Analysis/Diagnosis
Promotion: Prevention and
 Early Detection

5-17. A man has Huntington's disease. His son is exhibiting mild symptoms of the disorder. The son and his partner visit a genetic counselor to discuss the risk of their having a baby with Huntington's disease. The counselor correctly informs the couple that Huntington's disease is an example of autosomal dominant inheritance, and there is

a. a 50 percent chance that the abnormal gene will be passed on, but only to the male offspring.

b. approximately a 10 percent chance that the abnormal gene will be passed on to the offspring.

c. as high as a 50 percent possibility that the abnormal gene will be passed on to the offspring.

d. a 100 percent certainty that the affected parent will transmit the abnormal gene to the offspring.

d
Knowledge
Assessment
Promotion: Prevention and
 Early Detection

5-18. To assist a couple in understanding the transmission of an autosomal dominant inheritance, the genetic counselor constructs a graphic representation, called a

a. karyotype.

b. family graph.

c. genetic graph.

d. family pedigree.

a

Application

Analysis/Diagnosis

Physiological: Reduction of
  Risk Potential

5-19. A man has Huntington's disease and his son is exhibiting mild symptoms of the disorder. In order to eliminate any possibility of transmitting the disease to their offspring, the son and his partner are considering artificial insemination. Of the following, the best procedure would be to use

a. donor sperm, implanted in the woman.

b. the man's sperm, implanted in a gestational carrier.

c. the man's sperm, implanted in the partner after genetic restructuring.

d. donor sperm, implanted in a gestational carrier.

c

Comprehension

Analysis/Diagnosis

Physiological: Physiological
  Adaptation

5-20. A woman has cystic fibrosis. Because this is a condition of autosomal recessive inheritance, the nurse knows that the woman most likely inherited the disease from

a. her mother.

b. her father.

c. both parents.

d. neither.

d

Application

Planning

Physiological: Physiological
  Adaptation

5-21. A couple has a daughter with cystic fibrosis. The woman is pregnant, and the couple is concerned about the possibility of having another child with cystic fibrosis. Realizing that this is a condition of autosomal recessive inheritance, the nurse correctly gives them the information that

a. a female child would probably have the abnormal gene, but would only be a carrier.

b. it is almost certain that the baby will have cystic fibrosis.

c. it is very unlikely that any other children will be affected by the disease.

d. there is a 25 percent chance that the abnormal gene has been passed to the fetus.

c

Application

Implementation

Physiological: Physiological
  Adaptation

5-22. A couple has a son who has muscular dystrophy. They also have a daughter who is clinically well. They ask the pediatric nurse practitioner if there is a possibility that the daughter will transmit muscular dystrophy to her offspring. The nurse's correct response is, "This is an X-linked recessive disorder."

a. "Your daughter cannot pass the abnormal gene to her offspring since she does not have muscular dystrophy."

b. "Your daughter cannot pass the abnormal gene to her male offspring, but she may pass it her female offspring."

c. "There is a 50 percent chance that your daughter is a carrier and will pass the abnormal gene to her offspring."

d. "Your daughter is definitely a carrier of the abnormal gene, so there is a 50 percent chance that she will pass it to her offspring."

c

Application

Analysis/Diagnosis

Physiological: Physiological
    Adaptation

5-23. How is fragile X syndrome different from Down syndrome?
Fragile X syndrome

a. is an inherited form of mental retardation.

b. causes retardation in both males and females.

c. can be passed to offspring only by carrier mothers.

d. is a very common cause of mental retardation.

c

Knowledge

Assessment

Physiological: Physiological
    Adaptation

5-24. Sickle cell anemia, a condition that occurs primarily in the
African-American population, is an example of an inherited
disorder that is

a. multifactorial.

b. X-linked, recessive.

c. autosomal, recessive.

d. autosomal, dominant.

a

Knowledge

Assessment

Physiological: Physiological
    Adaptation

5-25. The product of the union of a normal gamete with a gamete
containing an extra chromosome results in

a. trisomy.

b. monosomy.

c. mosaicism.

d. translocation.

d

Comprehension

Analysis/Diagnosis

Physiological: Reduction of
    Risk Potential

5-26. What is an advantage of chorionic villus sampling (CVS)
when compared to amniocentesis? CVS

a. is less invasive.

b. is less expensive.

c. can be used for both infertility and genetic workups.

d. can be performed earlier in the pregnancy.

a

Knowledge

Assessment

Physiological: Physiological
    Adaptation

5-27. Down syndrome is an example of an abnormality of

a. an autosome.

b. a sex chromosome.

c. an autosome and a sex chromosome.

d. either an autosome or a sex chromosome.

c

Application

Planning

Physiological: Reduction of
    Risk Potential

5-28. As a part of an infertility evaluation, the nurse is scheduling a
client for a hysterosalpingogram to assess the patency of the
client's fallopian tubes. The nurse should explain to the client
that this will be done

a. just prior to menstrual period.

b. during menstrual period.

c. prior to ovulation.

d. immediately following ovulation.

a

Application

Planning

Safety: Management of Care

5-29. A couple wishes to have a baby and has been having unprotected intercourse for 6 months. The man is 45 and the woman is 40 years old. They should be referred for infertility evaluation

a. without further delay.

b. only if they are unsuccessful after another 3 months.

c. only if they are unsuccessful after another 6 months.

d. never, because of their ages.

a

Comprehension

Planning

Promotion: Growth and
    Development

5-30. A couple asks you, "Why is it that so many more couples are infertile these days?" How should you respond?

a. There has been no significant change in the incidence of infertility. It may seem higher for several reasons-for example, the increased availability and use of infertility services.

b. One reason is that more women are waiting until after age 35 to have babies.

c. The increased incidence of sexually transmitted diseases is the main cause of the increase in infertility.

d. Infertility is higher in women age 25-44, and this has caused an overall increase in the infertility rate.

c

Comprehension

Assessment

Promotion: Prevention and
    Early Detection

5-31. Screening by ultrasound for congenital anomalies is best done at 18-20 weeks' gestation. What is the rationale for this? At this stage

a. no harmful effects to the fetus have been documented.

b. there is an ample amount of amniotic fluid for visualization.

c. fetal structures have completed development and abnormalities can be visualized.

d. the sex of the fetus can be identified so that screening can be done for X-linked diseases.

d

Application

Analysis/Diagnosis

Physiological: Adaptation

5-32. How are Turner syndrome and Klinefelter syndrome *similar*? Both

a. result in mild mental retardation.

b. occur only in females and result in infertility.

c. occur because of an extra X chromosome.

d. result in underdeveloped secondary sex characteristics.

a

Knowledge

Assessment

Physiological: Physiological
    Adaptation

5-33. The genetic mechanism of diabetes mellitus is thought to be due to

a. a multifactorial inheritance trait.

b. an X-linked, dominant inheritance trait.

c. an autosomal, dominant inheritance trait.

d. an autosomal, recessive inheritance trait.

a

Application

Analysis/Diagnosis

Physiological: Physiological
    Adaptation

5-34. What do cleft palate, pyloric stenosis, spina bifida, and clubfoot have in common? They are

a. a result of multifactorial inheritance.

b. X-linked recessive disorders.

c. autosomal recessive disorders.

d. nongenetic conditions.

d

Application

Analysis/Diagnosis

Promotion: Prevention and
    Early Detection

5-35. A semen analysis reveals the following values: Volume = 2.5 ml, total sperm count = 15 million per mL; pH = 7.4; Motility = 65 percent. What is the correct conclusion to draw from this data?

a. All factors are within normal limits.

b. None of the factors is normal.

c. The semen volume is low.

d. The total sperm count is low.

c

Comprehension

Assessment

Physiological: Reduction of
    Risk Potential

5-36. When an infant with Down syndrome is born, the nursery nurse assesses for common dermatoglyphic patterns associated with this condition. These include

a. a decreased number of ulnar loops and 3 to 4 creases in the palm.

b. no visible loops on the finger tips and multiple creases in the palm.

c. a simian line in the palm and dermal ridge patterns.

d. lack of visible lines in the palm of the hand and an increase in radial loops on the fingertips.

Chapter 6
Preparing for Parenthood

a

Application

Planning

Promotion: Growth and
    Development

6-1. When making a birth plan, a client says, "One of my friends said that she had a whirlpool during her labor and it stopped her contractions. Do you think I should do that?" Which of the following would be the best response by the nurse?

a. "A whirlpool can provide pain relief; it won't slow your contractions if we don't use it too early in your labor."

b. "Actually, the whirlpool should stimulate rather than stop your labor. Your friend's experience was very unusual."

c. "If you want one, you can use a whirlpool at any time during labor, unless your membranes have ruptured."

d. "After your labor begins, we'll assess to see if a whirlpool is appropriate; if so, we'll ask your health care provider to order it."

b

Application

Implementation

Promotion: Growth and
    Development

6-2. A couple visits the obstetric clinic to discuss preparation for parenthood. They state, "We'd like to go to some prenatal classes, but we really don't know where to go." The nurse should reply

a. "I'll ask the doctor to recommend some classes for you."

b. "Perhaps I can help you find a class to meet your needs. Tell me a little more about what you have in mind."

c. "You probably won't need special classes if you make regular clinic visits. We will be able to answer your questions for you."

d. "You should go to the class at the hospital where you will deliver your baby. I'll call and schedule you, if you like."

a

Application

Implementation

Promotion: Growth and
    Development

6-3. A newly pregnant client states, "There are so many decisions to make, I don't even know where to start." The most appropriate nursing response would be

a. "Perhaps we could make a birth plan to help you decide issues such as type of childbirth preparation, place of birth, choice of the care provider, and activities during the birth."

b. "There are some decisions you will need to make; however, if you make a birth plan now, I can help you decide what to do about things like breastfeeding and activities during labor."

c. "Many decisions, such as activities during childbirth and type of childbirth preparation, are made by your care provider. You will need to make a few decisions, such as place of birth and choice of care provider."

d. "Don't be concerned about making decisions. Decision-making puts you in control of the situation so that the pregnancy and delivery will be less stressful to you."

d

Comprehension

Assessment

Promotion: Growth and
    Development

6-4. What do all antepartal education programs have in common? They

a. prepare the expectant couple for the labor experience.

b. relieve parents of their anxieties regarding labor.

c. promote the positive adjustment of siblings to the birth.

d. enhance the parents' decision-making skills.

a

Comprehension

Planning

Promotion: Growth and
    Development

6-5. A couple is expecting their first baby. The woman is one month pregnant and comes to the prenatal clinic for the first time. What should be included in the birth plan the nurse is helping her to devise?

a. identification of aspects of the childbearing experience that are most important to them

b. only the items/activities that are nonnegotiable

c. activities the couple have done to prepare themselves for childbirth

d. a statement indicating they accept responsibility for identifying options if the birth plan can't be followed

a

Comprehension

Evaluation

Promotion: Growth and
    Development

6-6. The nurse has helped a client devise a birth plan. What actions taken by the client would indicate appropriate use of the plan? She

a. shares the birth plan with the care provider and brings it to the birth setting when she is in labor.

b. understands how to develop the birth plan.

c. shares the plan with the nurse rather than with the care provider.

d. sends the plan to the care provider and waits for it to be brought up in conversation.

c

Comprehension

Planning

Promotion: Growth and
    Development

6-7. The nurse can best assist a couple with advance decisions about their birth experience by

a. recommending that they use an obstetrician rather than a general practitioner.

b. recommending that they use a midwife rather than an obstetrician.

c. helping them develop a list of questions to use in interviewing care providers.

d. explaining the complications that could occur in a home birth setting.

a

Application

Analysis/Diagnosis

Promotion: Growth and
    Development

6-8. A couple is trying to decide on a birth setting. They are seeking additional information from couples who have recently given birth. Which of the following questions should they ask their friends in order to elicit the most helpful information?

a. "Was your labor partner/coach treated well?"

b. "Were your labor and birth successful?"

c. "What medications did you take?"

d. "How long was your labor?"

b

Application

Planning

Promotion: Growth and
    Development

6-9. A couple has been married for 7 years; they have two children, a son who is 6 years old and a daughter who is 5 years old. The wife is 6 months pregnant, and the couple must make a decision about including the children in the birth experience. Which of the following principles should the nurse consider when preparing their teaching plan?

a. The decision to have children present at the birth should be based primarily on assessments made by the midwife during labor.

b. Children who will attend a birth should be prepared through books, audiovisual materials, models, and parental discussion.

c. Recent studies have demonstrated a slight increase in bacterial colonization rates in newborns when siblings are present.

d. During the labor and delivery process, the husband will need to focus on tending to the needs of the children.

b

Application

Planning

Promotion: Growth and
    Development

6-10. A couple has decided to have their two children, ages 5 and 6 years, present at the birth of the third child. An appropriate nursing intervention at the time of the birth would be to

a. suggest that the children stand at the foot of the bed for a better view.

b. allow the children to relate to the birth in whatever manner they choose, as long as it is not disruptive.

c. inform the children that they must stay in the room until the birth is over.

d. dress the children in surgical masks and gowns.

a

Comprehension

Planning

Promotion: Growth and
    Development

6-11. When scheduling the content for a series of childbirth preparation classes, the nurse should schedule information

a. in the order in which it occurs in pregnancy (e.g., present information about first trimester discomforts at an earlier session than the labor and delivery information).

b. about cesarean birth only if someone in the class is going to have a cesarean delivery.

c. only when it relates to problems the couples mention in class (e.g., discuss ways to relieve nausea when one of the women mentions she has been experiencing this problem).

d. so that the entire series of classes can be completed by the end of the second trimester.

b
Comprehension
Planning
Promotion: Growth and
    Development

6-12. The nurse is planning a first trimester prenatal class. Which of the following would be appropriate content? The nurse should include

a. infant care and feeding.

b. fetal development and sexuality in pregnancy.

c. medications and fetal monitoring.

d. safety issues regarding the newborn.

c
Comprehension
Planning
Promotion: Growth and
    Development

6-13. Which of the following should be included in the content of a third trimester childbirth preparation class?

a. effects of alcohol and smoking on the fetus

b. maternal-fetal nutrition

c. information about infant car seats

d. psychological changes in pregnancy

a
Comprehension
Planning
Promotion: Growth and
    Development

6-14. The *primary* purpose of relaxation during labor is to

a. allow the woman to conserve energy and allow the uterine muscles to work more efficiently.

b. strengthen the abdominal muscles for the expulsion phase of labor.

c. provide self-help measures so that the birth will be a healthy, happy event.

d. help keep the mother and unborn baby adequately oxygenated.

b
Comprehension
Implementation
Promotion: Growth and
    Development

6-15. A pregnant woman is practicing a relaxation exercise. She first contracts, then relaxes, various muscles throughout her body. Her partner checks her body for tense areas and reminds her to relax those body parts. For example, he says, "Contract right arm. Hold. Release." The couple is practicing an exercise known as

a. effleurage.

b. dissociation relaxation.

c. touch relaxation.

d. progressive relaxation.

d
Knowledge
Planning
Promotion: Growth and
    Development

6-16. The most useful content in prenatal classes for grandparents may well be

a. the tour of the birthing unit.

b. the discussion of sibling rivalry and adjustment.

c. information about the process of labor and birth.

d. changes in birthing and parenting practices.

a

Knowledge

Planning

Promotion: Growth and
    Development

6-17. Which of the childbirth preparation methods emphasizes "mind prevention" via education and training?

a. Lamaze

b. Bradley

c. hypnosis

d. Kitzinger

a

Application

Assessment

Physiological: Basic Care and
    Comfort

6-18. A woman is in the first stage of labor. During her contractions, she is stroking her abdomen in a circular motion with her hands. She is

a. doing this to relieve pain.

b. practicing a Bradley exercise.

c. using a method known as touch relaxation.

d. about to enter the transition stage.

b

Knowledge

Assessment

Promotion: Growth and
    Development

6-19. Preconception counselors are likely to suggest that a couple seek genetic counseling if the woman is over age

a. 25.

b. 35.

c. 40.

d. 45.

c

Comprehension

Planning

Promotion: Growth and
    Development

6-20. A couple is planning to have a child. The woman has been taking oral contraceptives. The nurse should counsel her to stop the pill

a. immediately when she wishes to become pregnant.

b. and wait six months before attempting to become pregnant.

c. and have two or three normal menses before attempting pregnancy.

d. at the end of her first period after deciding to attempt pregnancy.

b

Knowledge

Assessment

Physiological: Basic Care and
    Comfort

6-21. In which of the following exercises does firm, sensitive touch provide the stimulus for a woman to consciously release muscle tension while in labor?

a. effleurage

b. touch relaxation

c. progressive relaxation

d. dissociation relaxation

c
Comprehension
Planning
Promotion: Growth and
   Development

6-22. A couple has decided to have a doula during their birthing experience. The nurse would expect the doula to

a. provide support only when a nurse is not available.

b. encourage the father to leave the room from time to time to reduce his anxiety.

c. act as an advocate for the couple and verbalize their wishes to nurses and doctors.

d. take the client's vital signs and keep her perineum clean during labor.

b
Comprehension
Planning
Promotion: Growth and
   Development

6-23. A pregnant woman says to the nurse, "My friend had a midwife deliver her baby, but I really don't know who to get for that." The nurse can best help her by

a. referring her to a family practice physician or an obstetrician.

b. explaining the differences in the various primary care providers she might use.

c. suggesting that she ask a few other friends what kind of caregiver they had present at their births.

d. explaining that childbirth is a normal process, not an illness, and that both lay and certified midwives are qualified to attend a birth.

b
Application
Analysis/Diagnosis
Promotion: Growth and
   Development

6-24. A couple is visiting the obstetric clinic to discuss preparation for parenthood. In helping them decide what parent education classes to take, which of the following is the MOST important data for the nurse to have?

a. Is this their first pregnancy?

b. What do they want to learn about?

c. Will their insurance cover childbirth preparation classes?

d. What classes are available in the clinic?

b
Comprehension
Assessment
Promotion: Growth and
   Development

6-25. The nurse teaching a childbirth preparation class realizes that it is important to include information about preparing for cesarean birth because approximately 1 out of every _____ births is cesarean.

a. 5

b. 10

c. 25

d. 50

Chapter 7
Physiological and Psychological Changes of Pregnancy

b
Knowledge
Assessment
Promotion: Growth and
    Development

7-1. A multigravida may feel fetal movement as early as
    a. 12 weeks.
    b. 16 weeks.
    c. 20 weeks.
    d. 26 weeks.

a
Knowledge
Assessment
Promotion: Growth and
    Development

7-2. Which of the following physiological changes occurs in a pregnant woman?
    a. The joints of the pelvis relax.
    b. The cervix becomes pale and firm.
    c. The uterus doubles in size.
    d. Gastric emptying time is faster.

c
Application
Assessment
Promotion: Growth and
    Development

7-3. A pregnant woman is one week from delivery. Her nurse notes from the chart that her pulse was 74-80 bpm before she became pregnant. An expected finding for her on this visit would be a pulse of
    a. 60 beats/min.
    b. 70 beats/min.
    c. 90 beats/min.
    d. 100 beats/min.

b
Knowledge
Implementation
Promotion: Growth and
    Development

7-4. An RN instructs her client, at 24 weeks' gestation, to rest in a side-lying position and avoid lying flat on her back. The nurse explains that this is to avoid "supine hypotensive syndrome," a condition which
    a. occurs when blood pressure increases sharply with changes in position.
    b. results when blood flow returning from the extremities is blocked or slowed.
    c. is seen mainly in first pregnancies.
    d. may require medication if positioning does not help.

a
Comprehension
Assessment
Promotion: Growth and
    Development

7-5. During pregnancy the plasma volume increases to a greater extent than the number of red blood cells. This change results in
    a. physiologic anemia.
    b. physiologic leukocytosis.
    c. blood which clots more readily.
    d. a risk for thrombophlebitis.

a

Application

Analysis/Diagnosis

Promotion: Growth and
    Development

7-6. In the third trimester, a pregnant woman's total erythrocyte volume has increased by 15 percent; her leukocyte count is 10,000/mm^3. How should the nurse interpret these findings?

a. erythrocytes lower than expected; leukocytes normal

b. erythrocytes normal; leukocytes lower than expected

c. both erythrocytes and leukocytes higher than expected

d. both erythrocytes and leukocytes lower than expected

d

Application

Implementation

Promotion: Growth and
    Development

7-7. A client complains that during her first few months of pregnancy "it seems like I have to go to the bathroom every five minutes." The nurse should explain that this is because

a. she probably has a bladder or kidney infection.

b. bladder capacity normally increases throughout pregnancy.

c. women are sometimes very sensitive to their body functions during pregnancy.

d. the growing uterus puts pressure on the bladder.

b

Knowledge

Assessment

Promotion: Growth and
    Development

7-8. In pregnancy, the glomerular filtration rate

a. is directly influenced by the woman's posture.

b. increases significantly above prepregnant levels.

c. increases most during the third trimester.

d. changes only when pathological conditions are present.

d

Comprehension

Implementation

Promotion: Growth and
    Development

7-9. A client, who is in the second trimester of her pregnancy, tells the nurse that her sister developed large brown spots on her cheeks when she was pregnant. The client asks what other skin changes she might expect to see during her pregnancy. The nurse should tell the client that she might notice a

a. lightening of the nipples and areola of the breasts.

b. decreased tendency to sweat, along with skin dryness.

c. noticeable increase in the growth of her hair.

d. darkened line in the midline of her abdomen from the pubic symphysis to the umbilicus.

b

Comprehension

Implementation

Promotion: Growth and
    Development

7-10. At a prenatal visit a dipstick analysis of your client's urine shows a "trace" of glucose. When the client asks what that means, the nurse should reply

a. "We'll do a blood glucose test, and the doctor will talk to you about this later."

b. "This is a common finding that means the kidneys are not able to keep up with reabsorbing all the glucose."

c. "You may be developing gestational diabetes."

d. "You will need to increase your exercise in order to avoid glucose wasting."

a
Comprehension
Analysis/Diagnosis
Promotion: Growth and
    Development

7-11. A 22-year-old primigravida is 10 weeks pregnant. She says she has been nauseated periodically throughout the day for the last two weeks. The nurse understands that this common finding early in pregnancy is *primarily* due to

a. increased levels of hCG.

b. ambivalence about the pregnancy.

c. lateral displacement of the intestines.

d. sluggish intestinal peristalsis.

c
Knowledge
Assessment
Promotion: Growth and
    Development

7-12. "Probable" signs of pregnancy are those that are

a. reported by the woman.

b. considered to be diagnostic of pregnancy.

c. observable by the examiner.

d. found by use of ultrasound.

d
Comprehension
Implementation
Promotion: Growth and
    Development

7-13. A 19-year-old woman comes to the clinic after missing two menstrual periods. A Gravidex immunoassay pregnancy test is performed, and the client asks for information about the test. The nurse should reply that "Pregnancy tests such as this

a. take about one week to obtain the results."

b. are the most accurate pregnancy tests available today."

c. tell us for certain whether you are pregnant."

d. detect positive results 10 to 14 days after the first missed period."

a
Comprehension
Analysis/Diagnosis
Promotion: Growth and
    Development

7-14. Which of the following uses of ultrasound will enable the care provider to make the earliest positive diagnosis of pregnancy? Use ultrasound to

a. visualize the gestational sac.

b. hear the fetal heartbeat.

c. identify the uterine souffle.

d. recognize the signs of uterine vasocongestion.

a
Application
Analysis/Diagnosis
Promotion: Growth and
    Development

7-15. A 19-year-old woman is in the first trimester of her pregnancy. During the interview, you ask her partner a general question about how she has been lately. Which of the following is a typical response to pregnancy that you should expect him to report at this time? "She

a. is very body-conscious; she monitors every little change."

b. daydreams about how the baby will look and act after it is born."

c. asks her friends about their experiences with childbirth."

d. has been expressing concern about how she will act in labor."

c

Application

Analysis/Diagnosis

Psychosocial: Coping and
    Adaptation

7-16. Which of the following comments should cause the nurse to be concerned about a pregnant woman's emotional adaptation, and would warrant further assessment?

a. "I can't believe I'm pregnant. It doesn't seem real yet."

b. "We've wanted children, but I wish my husband could have finished college first."

c. "I never wanted to be pregnant; I don't want a baby."

d. "I'm as big as a barn. I feel so ugly."

a

Application

Planning

Promotion: Growth and
    Development

7-17. A primigravida in the first trimester of pregnancy asks you to recommend 1 or 2 good books for her to read on pregnancy and childbirth. You recognize that this activity will help the client to accomplish which of the following tasks of pregnancy?

a. safe passage for herself and the fetus through pregnancy, labor, and birth

b. acceptance of the unborn child by others

c. committing herself to mothering the infant

d. learning to accept her body in its present condition

c

Application

Planning

Promotion: Growth and
    Development

7-18. At a second trimester prenatal visit, a couple is discussing their new roles as parents with the nurse. The father comments that he really wants to be a good father to their new baby. The nurse should explain that in developing the fatherhood role the *most* important thing is to

a. participate actively in as many aspects of childbearing and childrearing as possible.

b. identify a father he admires and try to develop a fathering role similar to that.

c. decide with his partner on a fathering role that is mutually agreeable to both of them.

d. begin by examining the basic pattern of fathering that his father used with him.

b

Application

Implementation

Promotion: Growth and
    Development

7-19. A woman is 20 weeks pregnant. During a prenatal visit, she asks the nurse how she should prepare her 18-month-old son for the new baby. The nurse's best response would be

a. "Introduce the baby to him initially when you bring the baby home from the hospital."

b. "Begin several weeks before the baby is due; let him feel the baby move inside your abdomen."

c. "He should be included in every aspect of the pregnancy so that he will not feel excluded."

d. "Initiate an explanation of your pregnancy now rather than waiting for him to ask questions."

b

Application

Evaluation

Promotion: Growth and
    Development

7-20. A woman who is 20 weeks pregnant has an 18-month-old son. Following an extensive discussion of sibling rivalry, the nurse asks her to give some examples of how her son might be expected to behave when she brings the new baby home. If discussion has been effective in increasing her understanding, the client would reply

a. "He will ignore the new baby since he's really too young to understand what's going on."

b. "He may want to have a bottle or to climb into the baby's crib."

c. "He will be thrilled that he now has a new brother or sister to play with."

d. "He will feel important when I ask him to watch the baby while I do the dishes."

b

Application

Planning

Promotion: Growth and
    Development

7-21. A 23-year-old Philippine American is 18 weeks pregnant. After receiving a prescription for prenatal vitamins, she tells the nurse that her mother always warned her not to take any medications during pregnancy. The nurse's initial intervention should be to

a. remind Maria that the vitamins were ordered for her by the nurse midwife.

b. determine how important Maria's mother's advice is to her.

c. assure Maria that the pills are only vitamins and are not considered medication.

d. explain to Maria that her baby needs the vitamins in order to grow and be healthy.

c

Application

Analysis/Diagnosis

Promotion: Growth and
    Development

7-22. Which nurse is demonstrating ethnocentrism? One who thinks,

a. "I suppose the way I responded to that client was largely determined by my values, which have been shaped by my culture."

b. "I think every cultural group must have a core of beliefs that are common to every other culture."

c. "I realize that men of that culture make most family decisions, but she is really too submissive. I need to help her to be more assertive."

d. "The only way I'll be able to understand another person's culture is by looking at it from the perspective of my own culture."

a

Application

Implementation

Promotion: Growth and
    Development

7-23. A woman in the third trimester of pregnancy reports that she feels some lumpy places in her breasts and that they sometimes leak a yellowish fluid. The woman has an appointment with the nurse practitioner in two weeks. The nurse should

a. explain that this is normal, but can be assessed further when she comes in.

b. ask her if she has noticed a darkening of her areolae.

c. ask her if the fluid is more noticeable after intercourse.

d. suggest that she come in to be examined in a day or two instead of waiting until her appointment.

c

Knowledge

Analysis/Diagnosis

Promotion: Growth and
    Development

7-24. Which of the following is a positive sign (diagnostic) of pregnancy?

a. a positive radioreceptor assay (RRA) test

b. fetal movements felt by the pregnant woman

c. fetal heartbeat detected with a fetoscope

d. enlargement of the abdomen

a

Comprehension

Analysis/Diagnosis

Promotion: Growth and
    Development

7-25. When assessing the physical status of a woman of 10 weeks' gestation, which of the following *probable* signs of pregnancy would you expect to find?

a. bluish discoloration of the vagina and cervix

b. Braxton Hicks contractions

c. fetal heart tones

d. morning sickness

a

Application

Analysis/Diagnosis

Promotion: Growth and
    Development

7-26. A pregnant woman in her third trimester complains of nasal stuffiness and occasional nose bleeds. Her chest circumference has increased by 5 cm during the pregnancy, and she uses thoracic breathing. Her diaphragm is elevated and she has an increased subcostal angle. The nurse should

a. record that respiratory findings are normal.

b. ask another nurse to check the subcostal angle.

c. examine her for other signs of tissue anoxia (e.g., pallor).

d. have the physician evaluate her respiratory status.

b

Application

Implementation

Promotion: Growth and
    Development

7-27. A woman telephones the clinic to say that it has been six weeks since her last menstrual period, but that her home pregnancy test was negative today. She asks, "Do you think I could be pregnant?" After determining that the test was performed correctly, the nurse's best reply would be

a. "Probably not. These tests rarely give a false-negative result."

b. "You might be. If you haven't started your period in one week, you should repeat the test and call me again."

c. "You probably are. There are a lot of false-negative results with these tests."

d. "You may have an ectopic pregnancy. You should be seen by a doctor in the next few days."

d

Knowledge

Assessment

Promotion: Growth and
    Development

7-28. Of the hormones produced during pregnancy, which one is MOST significant in maintaining the pregnancy after the first trimester?

a. human chorionic gonadotropin

b. human placental lactogen

c. estrogen

d. progesterone

b

Application

Analysis/Diagnosis

Promotion: Growth and
    Development

7-29. A pregnant woman, at term, weighs 150 lb. Her prepregnant weight was 135 lb, which was normal for her height. The nurse has concluded that the woman did not eat enough during her pregnancy. Evaluate the nurse's conclusion. The conclusion is

a. accurate, justified, and well supported by the data.

b. suggested by the inadequate weight gain, but needs more data to confirm.

c. not at all justified, because the woman's weight gain was the recommended amount.

d. not at all justified, because the woman's weight gain was more than the recommended amount.

b

Knowledge

Assessment

Promotion: Growth and
    Development

7-30. The nurse can first palpate the fetal outline at what gestational age? Usually at

a. 12-16 weeks

b. 18-20 weeks

c. 24-26 weeks

d. 28-30 weeks

b
Knowledge
Assessment
Promotion: Growth and
    Development

7-31. The recommended total weight gain for a woman during pregnancy is
   a. the same, regardless of prepregnant weight.
   b. more for a normal than an overweight woman.
   c. more for a normal than an underweight woman.
   d. the same for a normal as an overweight woman.

a
Knowledge
Assessment
Promotion: Growth and
    Development

7-32. During pregnancy the capacity of the uterus increases from about 10 mL to 5 L or more. This is primarily a result of
   a. hypertrophy (increase in size) of the preexisting myometrial cells.
   b. hyperplasia (growth of new cells) of the myometrial cells.
   c. stretching from the growing uterine contents.
   d. an increase in fibrous tissue between the muscle bands.

Chapter 8
Antepartal Nursing Assessment

a

Knowledge

Assessment

Promotion: Growth and
   Development

8-1. A risk factor is a finding that has been shown to have a/an
   a. undesirable effect on the mother or the unborn child.
   b. undesirable effect on the mother.
   c. fatal effect on the unborn child.
   d. fatal effect on the mother or the unborn child.

a

Comprehension

Assessment

Promotion: Growth and
   Development

8-2. A woman has just given birth to a fetus at 18 weeks of gestation. The correct term for this is
   a. abortion.
   b. premature birth.
   c. fetal death.
   d. stillbirth.

a

Application

Assessment

Promotion: Growth and
   Development

8-3. When giving the obstetrical history, your client tells you that she has been pregnant twice before. She had a miscarriage with the first pregnancy after 8 weeks. With the second pregnancy, she delivered twin girls at 34 weeks' gestation, but the babies died two days after birth. The nurse should record that the client is
   a. gravida 3 para 1.
   b. gravida 3 para 0.
   c. gravida 3 para 2.
   d. gravida 2 para 3.

a

Application

Assessment

Promotion: Growth and
   Development

8-4. A client tells you she had a miscarriage with her first pregnancy after 8 weeks. With her second pregnancy, she delivered twin girls at 34 weeks' gestation, but the babies died two days after birth. Using the TPAL system to record her obstetrical history, the nurse should write
   a. gravida 3 para 0210.
   b. gravida 2 para 2012.
   c. gravida 3 para 0110.
   d. gravida 2 para 1100.

a

Application

Evaluation

Promotion: Prevention and
    Early Detection

8-5. Following the discussion on smoking and pregnancy, the
nurse asks the client to explain the effects of smoking on the
baby. Which of the following responses would indicate that
the client has learned correct information from the discussion?
"There is increased risk that the baby will have

a. a low birth weight."

b. a birth defect."

c. anemia."

d. nicotine withdrawal."

a

Application

Assessment

Health Promotion

8-6. A 17-year-old married client is 20 weeks pregnant, expecting
her first baby. In taking the prenatal history, which of the
following areas concerning her husband would be *especially*
important to assess?

a. occupation

b. drug allergies

c. childhood diseases

d. height and weight

b

Application

Analysis/Diagnosis

Promotion: Prevention and
    Early Detection

8-7. A 17-year-old primigravida is 20 weeks pregnant. She is 5
feet and 1 inch tall and weighs 212 pounds. The nurse should
realize that this weight puts her at increased risk for

a. cardiac decompensation.

b. cephalopelvic disproportion.

c. CNS irritability and convulsions.

d. postpartum infection.

b

Application

Analysis/Diagnosis

Promotion: Prevention and
    Early Detection

8-8. A primigravida is at 20 weeks gestation. Which of the
following physical assessment findings would necessitate
referral for further investigation?

a. spider nevi

b. 2+ ankle edema

c. fundus palpated at the umbilicus

d. odorless, cloudy, mucoid vaginal discharge

b

Comprehension

Analysis/Diagnosis

Promotion: Prevention and
    Early Detection

8-9. For a primigravida who is 20 weeks pregnant, which of the
following prenatal lab test results indicates an alteration from
expected normal findings?

a. hemoglobin 12.0 g/dL

b. rubella titer 1:8

c. white blood cell count 11,000

d. nonreactive VDRL

a

Application

Assessment

Promotion: Growth and
Development

8-10. A woman tells you that her last normal menstrual period was February 16. You would calculate her expected birthing date to be

a. November 23.

b. September 13.

c. December 28.

d. December 31.

a

Application

Assessment

Promotion: Growth and
Development

8-11. In addition to using your client's last menstrual period to determine her week of gestation, what other interview and/or physical examination data would you routinely use to validate the date?

a. Ask her if she has felt quickening, and if so, when it began.

b. Perform pelvimetry.

c. Check the x-ray for calcification of fetal bones.

d. Check for Chadwick's and Hegar's signs.

b

Comprehension

Assessment

Promotion: Prevention and
Early Detection

8-12. In assessing fundal height it is important for the nurse to

a. place the measuring tape at the top of the pubic arch.

b. have the client empty her bladder prior to the examination.

c. be aware that fundal height measurements correlate best with weeks of gestation after 32 weeks of pregnancy.

d. realize that maternal height does not affect the reading.

a

Application

Analysis/Diagnosis

Promotion: Growth and
Development

8-13. Using Naegle's rule, a woman is 26 weeks' gestation. She is moderately obese and carrying twins. The nurse measures her fundal height at 29 cm. The nurse should

a. recognize this as a reasonable measurement for this woman.

b. ask another nurse to confirm her measurement for accuracy.

c. realize that this may indicate intrauterine growth retardation.

d. recognize this as greater than expected and refer the information to the physician.

b

Knowledge

Assessment

Promotion: Growth and
Development

8-14. Which of the following measurements would a physician make vaginally in order to determine the adequacy of a woman's pelvis for birth?

a. true conjugate

b. diagonal conjugate

c. transverse outlet diameter

d. obstetrical conjugate

d
Comprehension
Analysis/Diagnosis
Promotion: Prevention and
    Early Detection

8-15. A pregnant client telephones the nurse to report some symptoms she is having. Which of the following symptoms should be reported to the client's physician immediately?

a. odorless, cloudy, mucoid vaginal discharge

b. urinary frequency

c. temperature of 37.8° C (100° F)

d. edema of the face and hands

d
Application
Analysis/Diagnosis
Promotion: Prevention and
    Early Detection

8-16. Which of the following third-trimester women would you suspect may be having difficulty with psychological adjustments to her pregnancy? One who

a. says, "Either a boy or a girl will be fine with me."

b. puts her feet up and listens to some music for 15 minutes when she is feeling too stressed.

c. was a smoker, but who has quit at least for the duration of her pregnancy.

d. has not investigated the kind of clothing or feeding methods the baby will need.

d
Comprehension
Assessment
Promotion: Growth and
    Development

8-17. A 26-year-old primipara is in her second trimester of pregnancy. Which of the following would be a part of a routine physical assessment for her third prenatal visit?

a. measurement of the diagonal conjugate

b. hepatitis B screening

c. complete blood count

d. measurement of fundal height

b
Application
Analysis/Diagnosis
Promotion: Prevention and
    Early Detections

8-18. When performing a prenatal assessment of parenting, which of the following comments would the nurse consider an indication of positive, prenatal, parental role development?

a. "We don't think we'll have to change our routine all that much after the baby is born."

b. "My partner is going to go to the childbirth preparation classes with me."

c. "I can't wait. It will be so nice to have a baby to love me."

d. "I'm sorry I missed my appointment again; I just get involved in what I'm doing and forget about it."

c

Application

Implementation

Promotion: Growth and
    Development

8-19. A woman and her partner are leaving the office after a second trimester prenatal visit. The man comments to the nurse, "I sometimes find it hard to talk to my wife. She seems to lost in her own thoughts much of the time." The nurse's most helpful initial response would be

a. "You will need to take the initiative in maintaining open communication."

b. "Do you think you are giving her enough attention?"

c. "Expectant fathers often feel this way during this time in the pregnancy."

d. "Don't worry about it; that's normal in pregnancy."

a

Application

Analysis/Diagnosis

Promotion: Prevention and
    Early Detection

8-20. A clinic nurse is performing an initial prenatal assessment. Which of the following findings should the nurse refer to the client's primary health care provider?

a. mottled skin and pallor of her palms and nail beds

b. spider nevi on her lower legs

c. dark pink, edematous nasal mucosa

d. mild enlargement of her thyroid gland

c

Application

Analysis/Diagnosis

Promotion: Prevention and
    Early Detection

8-21. When doing a prenatal assessment of parenting, which of the following comments by a woman would the nurse recognize as needing further investigation?

a. "I have so much to learn about taking care of a baby. I've bought a couple of books already."

b. "When will I be able to feel my baby move?"

c. "I work and have an active social life; I don't see how a baby will change it all that much."

d. "We've already told our parents we're expecting; and the people at work, too."

c

Application

Analysis/Diagnosis

Promotion: Growth and
    Development

8-22. For a woman in her first trimester of pregnancy, which of the following findings in a psychosocial assessment indicates an *alteration* from expected normal findings?

a. identifies at least 3 people with whom she feels very comfortable.

b. asks numerous questions regarding the pregnancy.

c. expresses marked anxiety over the diagnosis of pregnancy.

d. states that her husband has been employed as a cook for 2 years.

a

Comprehension

Assessment

Promotion: Growth and
    Development

8-23. A woman is pregnant for the first time. When you write up your prenatal assessment on her chart, you should refer to her as a

a. primigravida.

b. nulligravida.

c. primipara.

d. multipara.

d

Application

Analysis/Diagnosis

Promotion: Growth and
    Development

8-24. On a primigravida's second prenatal visit, at 15 weeks' gestation, the nurse continues the psychosocial assessment begun at the first visit. Which of the following questions would be most appropriate for the nurse to ask at this time?

a. "What preparations have you and your partner made at home for the baby?"

b. "Have you enrolled in prenatal classes yet?"

c. "Are you planning to have a medicated or an unmedicated birth?"

d. "What body changes have you noticed since your last visit?"

c

Knowledge

Implementation

Promotion: Growth and
    Development

8-25. Your client notices that you have written the word "multigravida" in her chart and she asks you what it means. You should reply, "Multigravida means

a. that you are pregnant."

b. the first weeks of gestation."

c. a woman experiencing her second or more pregnancy."

d. a woman who has had two or more births at more than 20 weeks' gestation."

b

Application

Analysis/Diagnosis

Promotion: Growth and
    Development

8-26. A 17-year-old primigravida is 20 weeks pregnant. At the clinic, her nurse performs a prenatal examination and obtains the following vital signs. Which finding should the nurse recognize as abnormal?

a. pulse 88/min

b. respirations 30/min

c. temperature 37.4° C (99.3° F)

d. blood pressure 134/86

Chapter 9
The Expectant Family: Needs and Care

c

Comprehension

Analysis/Diagnosis

Promotion: Growth and
  Development

9-1. A woman who is 30 weeks pregnant tells you that she has been having a strong, sharp, "catching" pain in her lower abdomen and groin area from time to time. You should explain to her that this sensation is probably due to

a. exaggerated Braxton-Hicks contractions.

b. developing urinary tract infection.

c. stretching of the round ligament.

d. pressure of the fetal head on the pelvic nerves.

b

Knowledge

Implementation

Promotion: Prevention and
  Early Detection

9-2. A pregnant woman tells the nurse, "I smoke a pack of cigarettes every day. Will smoking hurt my baby?" The nurse's best reply would be,

a. "A pack a day is excessive during pregnancy; you should cut back before the second trimester."

b. "It is best not to smoke at all, especially during pregnancy; smoking creates a number of risks for your baby."

c. "Yes it will. If you love your baby, you must quit smoking while you are pregnant."

d. "It won't hurt your baby directly, but it decreases your appetite, so you and the baby won't be as well nourished."

d

Application

Analysis/Diagnosis

Promotion: Prevention and
  Early Detection

9-3. A client at 16 weeks' gestation smokes cigarettes. She says, "I've managed to cut back from a pack and a half a day to a little over a half a pack a day, but I don't think I can do any better. I'm jittery and yelling at everybody." The nurse's most supportive and accurate reply would be,

a. "Any smoking is bad for your baby, and may even cause you to lose the baby. You must find a way to give it up."

b. "Good for you! A half a pack a day shouldn't be too bad for your baby, especially if you use filters to decrease the carbon monoxide. That's the worst ingredient."

c. "You've done well. Let's talk to the doctor about getting a nicotine patch for you for the rest of your pregnancy."

d. "Great! Any decrease in smoking reduces the risks to your baby. Try to maintain, and if you can, cut back more when you feel able."

a
Knowledge
Assessment
Promotion: Growth and
    Development

9-4. Nasal congestion and fullness ("stuffy nose") in pregnancy is caused by increased levels of

    a. estrogen.

    b. progesterone.

    c. chorionic gonadotropin.

    d. prolactin.

d
Comprehension
Planning
Physiological: Basic Care and
    Comfort

9-5. In order to relieve her nasal congestion you would suggest to a pregnant woman that she

    a. ask her physician to prescribe a decongestant.

    b. use a commercial nasal spray twice each day.

    c. use a hot steam vaporizer during the night.

    d. use a cool-air vaporizer.

d
Application
Analysis/Diagnosis
Physiological:
    Pharmacological and
    Parenteral

9-6. A client comments, "I know I'm not supposed to take medications while I'm pregnant, but I just have to take acetaminophen sometimes when I have a headache." Knowing that acetaminophen is a "Category B" drug, the nurse should reply "Acetaminophen

    a. increases the risk for congenital heart defects in your baby; you should not use it."

    b. may cause bleeding problems in the baby; don't use it in your third trimester."

    c. does have some minor risk to the baby, but in this case the benefits seem to outweigh the risk."

    d. is safe for occasional use, taken as directed; but it's safest to avoid taking any medications during pregnancy if you can."

a
Comprehension
Planning
Promotion: Growth and
    Development

9-7. In providing anticipatory guidance to a client regarding discomfort she might expect during the second trimester of pregnancy, you should include mention of

    a. hemorrhoids.

    b. nose bleeds.

    c. urinary frequency.

    d. increased vaginal discharge.

b
Comprehension
Evaluation
Physiological:
    Pharmacological and
    Parenteral

9-8. Sodium bicarbonate is not recommended for heartburn in pregnancy because it can

    a. lead to hypocalcemia.

    b. cause electrolyte imbalance.

    c. increase the symptoms of heartburn.

    d. destroy certain vitamins needed for fetal development.

b
Comprehension
Planning
Promotion: Growth and
    Development

9-9. To relieve heartburn, you would suggest to a pregnant woman that she might try

a. cutting down on the number of meals she eats.

b. avoiding fried foods in her diet.

c. not eating anything 2 or 3 hours before bedtime.

d. lying down after she eats.

c
Application
Implementation
Promotion: Growth and
    Development

9-10. A multipara mentions that her mother had "terrible varicose veins" with her pregnancies. She asks you if she will get them too. Your most appropriate response is,

a. "If you control your weight you won't have to worry about getting varicose veins."

b. "If you're worried about developing varicose veins, you should stop wearing panty hose."

c. "Heredity is a factor, but there are several other things that contribute to the development of varicose veins."

d. "Since you didn't develop varicose veins with your other pregnancies, you're not likely to have them with this one."

b
Comprehension
Evaluation
Promotion: Prevention and
    Early Detection

9-11. A client would demonstrate accurate knowledge of the prevention and treatment of varicose veins if she says she will avoid which of the following?

a. elastic stockings

b. prolonged standing

c. strenuous exercise

d. wearing panty hose

a
Application
Evaluation
Promotion: Growth and
    Development

9-12. A multipara who is 26 weeks pregnant has decided to change her method of exercise. Which of the following new activities would indicate that she understands how to exercise appropriately in late pregnancy?

a. swimming

b. ice skating

c. playing cards

d. tennis

a
Comprehension
Planning
Promotion: Prevention and
Early Detection

9-13. While discussing the topic of safety hazards during pregnancy, the nurse should instruct the second trimester gravida to avoid or use caution with which of the following activities?

a. taking tub baths, especially in very warm water

b. wearing a seat belt across her pelvis while driving

c. continuing her job as a secretary for a local insurance agency

d. receiving immunizations made from live attenuated organisms

d
Application
Planning
Promotion: Growth and
Development

9-14. A 20-year-old in the last trimester of pregnancy tells the nurse she has had trouble sleeping the last several nights. After assessing the client's sleeping habits, the nurse recommends that she

a. drink a cup of hot chocolate or tea just before going to bed.

b. exercise before going to bed so she will be tired and sleep well.

c. ask her physician to order sleeping pills for her.

d. use several pillows to support her body in positions of rest.

a
Application
Planning
Promotion: Growth and
Development

9-15. The client, in the third trimester of pregnancy, mentions that she sometimes feels faint. The nurse should instruct her that when signs of fainting appear, her first action should be to

a. sit down and lower her head.

b. get some fresh air.

c. call her physician.

d. breathe slowly into a paper bag.

c
Application
Planning
Promotion: Prevention and
Early Detection

9-16. A client is in the last trimester of her pregnancy. She and her partner would like to take a trip together before the baby is born. Which of the following responses by the nurse is MOST appropriate?

a. "Air travel after the second trimester is not advised."

b. "You should not plan to go more than 100 miles away."

c. "Be sure to stop every 2 hours when traveling by car."

d. "Foreign travel should be avoided during pregnancy."

a
Comprehension
Planning
Promotion: Growth and
Development

9-17. When establishing nursing care priorities for a pregnant woman, which of the following has the highest priority?

a. the safety of the fetus

b. the concerns of the woman

c. the integrity of the family unit

d. the physician's treatment plan

c
Application
Implementation
Promotion: Growth and
    Development

9-18. A client in her first trimester of pregnancy telephones the clinic to say that she has been nauseated every morning, and sometimes vomits. The nurse should advise her to

a. not eat between her regular 3 meals a day.

b. come to the clinic within the next day or two for an antiemetic.

c. call her physician if she vomits more than once a day and has scanty urine.

d. take some baking soda in water upon arising each morning.

c
Application
Analysis/Diagnosis
Promotion: Growth and
    Development

9-19. A client telephones to say that she is having an increased whitish vaginal discharge. The nurse tells her that this is normal during pregnancy. Evaluate the nurse's comment. It is

a. justified, on the basis of the data given.

b. not justified, on the basis of the data given.

c. possibly justified, but more data is needed.

d. factually incorrect; this is not normal.

a
Application
Planning
Safety: Management of Care

9-20. A Korean client cannot speak any English. The most effective nursing intervention during her pregnancy would be to

a. have an interpreter present at all clinic visits.

b. speak slowly to her, using short, simple words.

c. use pictures and drawings for food, water, pain, and so forth.

d. make eye contact when speaking to her, and give her written instructions.

b
Application
Analysis/Diagnosis
Promotion: Growth and
    Development

9-21. A client in her 12th week of pregnancy states that she is tired all the time. She says, "I have to have a nap after lunch, and I just fall into bed at night." The nurse's best response would be,

a. "Most pregnant women experience those symptoms."

b. "These symptoms are normal. They should go away in a week or two."

c. "Do you have to get up during the night to go to the bathroom?"

d. "Does your husband understand that he should help out more?"

a
Knowledge
Planning
Promotion: Growth and
    Development

9-22. For women with low risk pregnancies, prenatal care is usually

a. community based.

b. home based.

c. self administered.

d. provided by hospitals.

b
Comprehension
Analysis/Diagnosis
Safety: Management of Care

9-23. For which woman would antepartal home care be especially effective? One who has no
a. insurance.
b. transportation.
c. risk factors.
d. job.

a
Application
Analysis/Diagnosis
Physiological: Reduction of
    Risk Potential

9-24. What do nicotine and alcohol have in common? Both
a. are teratogens.
b. increase the incidence of infertility.
c. have neurologic effects on the fetus.
d. have been linked to sudden infant death syndrome.

b
Knowledge
Planning
Promotion: Prevention and
    Early Detection

9-25. For a normal pregnancy, when is sexual intercourse contraindicated?
a. during the last six weeks of pregnancy
b. after the membranes are ruptured
c. after fetal movements are felt
d. not at any time

a
Application
Implementation
Promotion: Prevention and
    Early Detection

9-26. A 39-year-old woman and her partner are expecting their first baby. They tell the nurse they have been thinking about having an amniocentesis. An *initial* response by the nurse should be,
a. "Tell me what you know about this procedure."
b. "That is a good idea. At your age you're at higher risk for developing problems."
c. "That will save you a lot of worry. You'll know today if your baby is normal or not."
d. "Why don't you think it over for a while? Wait a few weeks to make up your minds."

b
Application
Planning
Psychosocial: Coping and
    Adaptation

9-27. A 39-year-old woman has had an amniocentesis. When she and her partner return to the clinic 2 weeks later, they are told that test results indicate their fetus has Down syndrome. After allowing time for them to express their feelings about this information, the nurse should next
a. refer them to a genetic counselor.
b. provide them with information about Down syndrome.
c. help prepare them emotionally for an elective abortion.
d. assure them that many children with Down syndrome live nearly normal lives.

d

Application

Planning

Physiological: Basic Care and
    Comfort

9-28. A woman at 30 weeks' gestation says she has been having an occasional, intense "grabbing" pain low in her abdomen. She says that the physician has ruled out any medical complications. The best advice to the client is,

a. "There really isn't much you can do to relieve it."

b. "If it keeps you awake at night, you might try taking one acetaminophen tablet."

c. "Wearing a maternity girdle should help."

d. "It may help to use a heating pad on your abdomen."

c

Knowledge

Assessment

Promotion: Growth and
    Development

9-29. A 37-year-old client tells the clinic nurse that she is concerned about the possibility of having a baby with Down syndrome. The nurse responds that the incidence of Down syndrome for her would be about

a. 1 in 1000.

b. 1 in 600.

c. 1 in 200.

d. 1 in 50.

c

Application

Planning

Physiological:
    Pharmacological and
    Parenteral

9-30. The over-the-counter medications a pregnant client has been taking are in Category A of the Food and Drug Administration's classification system for medications administered in pregnancy. The nurse should

a. inform her of the risks associated with the medication.

b. monitor her baby's well-being by counting fetal movements at home.

c. reassure her that the medication is safe to take during pregnancy.

d. reassure her that studies have not proven risk, but that she should not take the medication during the remainder of her pregnancy.

a

Knowledge

Planning

Promotion: Prevention and
    Early Detection

9-31. Which exercise should be prescribed for reducing back strain in pregnancy?

a. pelvic tilt

b. partial sit-ups

c. Kegel's exercise

d. tailor sitting

c

Application

Planning

Promotion: Growth and
    Development

9-32. The nurse is teaching a primigravida client how to monitor fetal well-being by counting her baby's movements. The nurse should tell the client to notify her health care provider if she counts

a. fewer than 10 movements per hour.

b. more than 10 movements per hour.

c. fewer than 10 movements in 3 hours.

d. more than 10 movements in 3 hours.

c

Application

Planning

Physiological: Reduction of
    Risk Potential

9-33. A 24-year-old primigravida is in the first trimester of pregnancy. She complains, "I have to go to the bathroom a lot more these days." The nurse explains that this is common in early pregnancy, but that it can indicate a problem if the frequency is accompanied by

a. vulvar varicosities.

b. fatigue and the need to nap every day.

c. burning on urination, or a sense of urgency.

d. leakage of urine with coughing or sneezing.

d

Application

Analysis/Diagnosis

Promotion: Prevention and
    Early Detection

9-34. A pregnant woman tells the nurse, "I usually drink 2 glasses of wine with dinner. That doesn't sound too excessive does it?" Which of the following replies by the nurse is both caring and correct?

a. "You should limit your alcohol consumption to one glass of wine in the evening. Research shows that light drinking won't hurt your baby"

b. "The latest research shows that even light drinking increases the risks to your baby. You should not drink at all during pregnancy."

c. "It should be okay. Research shows that moderate drinking during pregnancy does not increase the risks to your baby."

d. "You should try not to drink at all. There is no proof that an occasional drink is harmful; still, no safe level of drinking during pregnancy has been identified."

Chapter 10
Adolescent Pregnancy

a

Knowledge

Assessment

Promotion: Prevention and
    Early Detection

10-1. Which method of birth control is most likely to be used by teenagers?

a. condoms

b. oral contraceptives

c. intrauterine devices

d. the rhythm method

b

Comprehension

Analysis/Diagnosis

Promotion: Prevention and
    Early Detection

10-2. A 16-year-old girl is pregnant. Her family is poor and they live in a run-down neighborhood. If she follows statistical norms, you would expect that the father of her child is

a. age 25, has a good job and lives in the suburbs.

b. age 17, unemployed and a high-school dropout.

c. age 35, married and owns an advertising agency.

d. age 16, in school and living with middle-class parents.

c

Comprehension

Analysis/Diagnosis

Promotion: Prevention and
    Early Detection

10-3. What contributes to the high incidence of teen pregnancy in the United States? Possible explanations have included the fact that adolescent girls

a. are comfortable with their sexuality.

b. are by nature optimistic about the future.

c. experience peer pressure to become sexually active.

d. perceive their locus of control as being internal.

c

Comprehension

Analysis/Diagnosis

Promotion: Prevention and
    Early Detection

10-4. A 16-year-old girl has had her pregnancy confirmed. Compared to a young adult woman, the client is at higher risk for having

a. a cesarean birth.

b. gestational diabetes.

c. a low birth weight baby.

d. placenta previa.

d

Application

Implementation

Promotion: Growth and
    Development

10-5. A woman brings her 15-year-old daughter to the prenatal clinic, where it is confirmed that the girl is pregnant. She asks, "What about my daughter's boyfriend? He's the father of this baby. What should I do about him?" The nurse's best response would include which of the following?

a. "Since they are both so young, it might be best if your daughter does not see him again."

b. Many teenage fathers don't want to continue the relationship once they know there is a pregnancy."

c. "You may need to remind him that he is legally obligated to support this baby."

d. "He may be a source of emotional support to Sara during the pregnancy."

c

Comprehension

Assessment

Promotion: Growth and
    Development

10-6. A nurse midwife determines that a 13-year-old girl is pregnant. If she is a typical 13-year-old, on whom will she rely when making decisions about whether to terminate her pregnancy, give the baby up for adoption, keep the baby, and so forth?

a. her peers

b. herself

c. her parents

d. her nurse

a

Comprehension

Analysis/Diagnosis

Promotion: Growth and
    Development

10-7. Which of the following pregnant adolescents is most likely to become pregnant a second time while still an adolescent? One who is

a. 13 years old.

b. 15 years old.

c. 17 years old.

d. 19 years old.

b

Knowledge

Assessment

Promotion: Growth and
    Development

10-8. The major psychologic risk to a pregnant adolescent is

a. rejection by her partner.

b. interruption in completing her developmental tasks.

c. that she may become severely depressed.

d. inability to form lasting relationships.

c
Knowledge
Analysis/Diagnosis
Safety: Management of Care

10-9. When giving a 15-year-old emancipated primigravida information about her pregnancy and condition, the nurse should know that the client's

a. parents have a right to all information about their daughter.

b. boyfriend, the father of the child, is the only one who should have access to this information.

c. parents should receive this information only if she agrees.

d. parents have no legal right to the information, but should be told for ethical reasons.

a
Comprehension
Analysis/Diagnosis
Promotion: Prevention and
    Early Detection

10-10. In order to assess for the most prevalent medical complication of adolescent pregnancy, the nurse would check the client's

a. blood pressure.

b. urine glucose level.

c. syphilis test results.

d. fetal heart rate.

b
Knowledge
Planning
Promotion: Growth and
    Development

10-11. Which of the following approaches would be BEST for prenatal teaching of pregnant teenagers?

a. Private, one-to-one counseling by the nurse

b. Age-appropriate audiovisual materials

c. Lectures in a group setting

d. The same teaching methods used for regular prenatal classes

d
Comprehension
Analysis/Diagnosis
Promotion: Growth and
    Development

10-12. Of the following, the nurse's most important *initial* responsibility in teaching the pregnant adolescent is to

a. advise her about proper care of the infant.

b. instruct her about danger signs of pregnancy-induced hypertension.

c. instruct her about special concerns of pregnancy.

d. motivate her to attend clinic appointments regularly.

a
Comprehension
Analysis/Diagnosis
Promotion: Growth and
    Development

10-13. Which of the following statements is CORRECT about the early adolescent who becomes pregnant?

a. She is a concrete thinker and may have difficulty anticipating the consequences of sexual activity.

b. She wants to be treated like an adult and begins to seek adult responsibilities and pleasures.

c. She is comfortable with her personal identity but is susceptible to peer pressure.

d. She has an internalized locus of control and can make abstract choices.

d
Comprehension
Assessment
Promotion: Growth and
    Development

10-14. What is the most critical factor in producing positive outcomes for the adolescent mother and her baby?

a. the girl's age

b. having supportive parents

c. a stable financial situation

d. early, good prenatal care

d
Comprehension
Planning
Promotion: Growth and
    Development

10-15. When is the best time to teach a 15-year-old girl about parenting and childcare?

a. second trimester

b. third trimester

c. during latent labor

d. after the baby is born

c
Comprehension
Analysis/Diagnosis
Promotion: Growth and
    Development

10-16. Compared to children of adult parents, the children of adolescent parents are less likely to

a. be sexually active in adolescence.

b. have behavior problems.

c. do well in school.

d. abuse drugs.

c
Knowledge
Assessment
Promotion: Growth and
    Development

10-17. Which of the following is a developmental task of adolescence?

a. Developing trust in others.

b. Developing a sense of continuity.

c. Developing intimacy in a relationship.

d. Developing productivity and concern for others.

c
Knowledge
Assessment
Promotion: Growth and
    Development

10-18. For a girl younger than 15 years, who is usually the best source of support during pregnancy and childbirth? Her

a. boyfriend.

b. girlfriends.

c. mother.

d. father.

a
Knowledge
Analysis/Diagnosis
Promotion: Growth and
    Development

10-19. Compared to older partners of adolescent mothers, adolescent partners tend to

a. marry younger.

b. have smaller families.

c. provide less financial support.

d. be less likely to get a divorce.

d
Comprehension
Assessment
Promotion: Prevention and
    Early Detection

10-20. When a very young adolescent becomes pregnant, it is especially important to

a. involve the sexual partner in the pregnancy and support the relationship.

b. gradually require the adolescent to assume independent decision-making.

c. refer her for therapeutic abortion counseling.

d. assess for incest or sexual abuse.

c
Knowledge
Assessment
Promotion: Prevention and
    Early Detection

10-21. Compared to Japan and industrialized European nations, in the United States the incidence of teenage

a. sexual activity is about the same.

b. sexual activity is lower.

c. pregnancy is higher.

d. pregnancy is about the same.

Chapter 11
Maternal Nutrition

d

Application

Assessment

Promotion: Growth and
    Development

11-1. A pregnant 14-year-old is 2 years past menarche. Her prepregnant weight is average for her height. Her optimum total weight gain during pregnancy would be

a. 20 lbs.

b. 25 lbs.

c. 30 lbs.

d. 35 lbs.

a

Application

Assessment

Promotion: Growth and
    Development

11-2. A 16-year-old girl is pregnant. She began menstruating when she was 11 years old. Her weight is average for her height. Compared to a 25-year-old pregnant woman of the same weight and height, the teenager's calorie needs during pregnancy are

a. about the same.

b. slightly higher.

c. significantly higher.

d. lower.

c

Knowledge

Analysis/Diagnosis

Promotion: Growth and
    Development

11-3. Which of the following is normal during pregnancy?

a. increased elimination of fat through the bowel

b. a decrease in serum lipoproteins and cholesterol

c. more complete absorption of ingested fats

d. fat deposits in the fetus of about 20 percent to 30 percent

a

Comprehension

Planning

Physiological:
    Pharmacological and
    Parenteral

11-4. In order to prevent gastrointestinal upset, you should advise clients to take iron supplements

a. after a meal.

b. before eating.

c. before bedtime.

d. first thing in the morning.

a

Comprehension

Planning

Promotion: Prevention and
    Early Detection

11-5. A client's first child had spina bifida (a neural tube defect). Therefore, during this pregnancy her physician will probably recommend large dose supplementation of

a. folic acid.

b. protein.

c. iron.

d. calcium.

c
Comprehension
Planning
Promotion: Growth and
    Development

11-6. A pregnant woman following a vegan diet will need to choose and combine foods carefully, especially in order to provide sufficient
a. vitamin C.
b. folic acid.
c. calories.
d. vitamin B.

c
Comprehension
Implementation
Promotion: Growth and
    Development

11-7. The client states, "I have heard that a pregnant woman needs more iron. Is that true?" The nurse's best response should be,
a. "Yes, a pregnant woman, age 23 to 40, needs 50 percent more iron."
b. "Yes, but the increase is so small a pregnant woman can meet the need by eating a well-balanced diet."
c. "Yes, a pregnant woman needs about twice as much iron."
d. "Only pregnant adolescents have an increased need for iron."

b
Comprehension
Analysis/Diagnosis
Promotion: Prevention and
    Early Detection

11-8. A client states, "I don't really like to drink milk." Which of the following foods should the nurse recommend to her?
a. cottage cheese, dry cereal, orange juice
b. cheese, yogurt, custard pudding
c. ice cream, eggs, hot cakes
d. powdered milk, artificial cheese, peanut butter

d
Comprehension
Planning
Promotion: Growth and
    Development

11-9. A 28-year-old woman has just had her pregnancy confirmed. She is particularly concerned about weight gain. The nurse should tell her that
a. all pregnant women should gain at least 20 lbs.
b. research has shown that the amount of weight gained is not important; it is the pattern of gain that matters.
c. underweight women should not expect to gain as much weight as women of normal weight.
d. the optimal amount of weight gain depends on factors such as height and bone structure.

c
Knowledge
Planning
Promotion: Growth and
    Development

11-10. For a woman of normal weight, the nurse is writing a goal based on Institute of Medicine Guidelines, which specify an average total weight gain of
a. 10 to 15 lbs.
b. 16 to 20 lbs.
c. 25 to 35 lbs.
d. 35 to 40 lbs.

a
Comprehension
Evaluation
Promotion: Growth and
    Development

11-11. A woman, age 28, is of average weight and height. The nurse would evaluate that she is meeting her ideal nutritional goals if she gains _____ during the first trimester of pregnancy.

a. 3.5 to 5 lbs

b. 5 to 10 lbs

c. 1 lb per week

d. less than 2 lbs

d
Knowledge
Assessment
Promotion: Growth and
    Development

11-12. For a woman of normal weight, the goal for weight gain during the last 2 trimesters of pregnancy should be

a. 4 lbs. per week

b. 3 lbs. per week

c. 2 lbs. per week

d. 1 lb. per week

a
Application
Analysis/Diagnosis
Promotion: Growth and
    Development

11-13. A client visits the clinic during the eleventh week of pregnancy. She has gained 4 pounds above her normal pre-pregnant weight. What is the best interpretation of this data?

a. This weight gain is appropriate and the client should be commended for her eating pattern.

b. This small weight gain puts her at risk for intrauterine growth retardation.

c. This large weight gain puts her at risk for pre-eclampsia.

d. Observation of weight trends for several months is needed to assess adequate weight gain.

a
Comprehension
Assessment
Promotion: Prevention and
    Early Detection

11-14. Women who are 10 percent or more below their recommended weight prior to conception a have an increased probability ofh

a. delivering a low birth weight infant.

b. remaining at optimal weight throughout the entire pregnancy.

c. developing anemia during pregnancy.

d. developing calcium depletion during pregnancy.

b
Application
Planning
Promotion: Growth and
    Development

11-15. A woman is 16 weeks pregnant, moderately active, and weighs 132 pounds. In her second trimester, she will need to add approximately _____ calories per day to her diet.

a. 100

b. 300

c. 500

d. 1000

b
Comprehension
Implementation
Promotion: Growth and
    Development

11-16. The client asks, "Why is protein so important during pregnancy?" The nurse should explain, "Protein is necessary for
a. development of fetal teeth and bones."
b. growth of fetal and maternal tissues."
c. prevention of anemia."
d. its carbohydrate-sparing action."

c
Application
Analysis/Diagnosis
Promotion: Growth and
    Development

11-17. On a previous visit, the nurse discussed food sources and the importance of protein-rich foods with a client. She will evaluate that learning occurred if the client tells her she has been eating
a. carrots, peas, and enriched bread.
b. whole wheat bread, butter, and spinach greens.
c. eggs, pork chops, macaroni and cheese.
d. dried fruits, molasses, and cornbread.

c
Comprehension
Analysis/Diagnosis
Promotion: Growth and
    Development

11-18. A teaching plan to assure that the client is eating sufficient carbohydrates would include teaching her to choose
a. chicken, tuna, and eggs.
b. liver, ham, and tomatoes.
c. apples, corn, and bread.
d. boiled eggs, catfish, and broccoli.

b
Comprehension
Analysis/Diagnosis
Promotion: Growth and
    Development

11-19. When counseling a client about foods high in iron, which of the following meals would you recommend to her?
a. tuna sandwich, chocolate pudding, fruit salad
b. shrimp, tossed green salad, dried apricots
c. omelet, raw apple, spinach salad
d. hamburger, french fries, fruit cup

a
Application
Analysis/Diagnosis
Physiological: Physiological
    Adaptation

11-20. A 14-year-old client has just had her pregnancy confirmed. During the initial assessment, she states that she has been having abdominal distention, generalized discomfort, nausea, loose stools and cramps. These symptoms have existed for years and are recurring in nature. The nurse should
a. ask her whether her symptoms are associated with drinking milk or eating foods containing milk.
b. ask her if her symptoms are associated with exercise.
c. obtain the results of her serum chemical 25 survey.
d. obtain the results from her abdominal CAT scan.

a
Comprehension
Planning
Promotion: Prevention and
    Early Detection

11-21. A 14-year-old pregnant client comments that she does not like milk. This may mean that she will need

a. a calcium supplement.

b. an iron supplement.

c. to eat more frequent meals.

d. to increase her calorie intake.

a
Comprehension
Planning
Promotion: Prevention and
    Early Detection

11-22. Of course, all nutrients and vitamins must be considered when evaluating a pregnant teenager's diet. Which of the following, though, is especially indicated for a pregnant adolescent? A/an

a. iron supplement.

b. calcium supplement.

c. low dose vitamin supplement.

d. large increase in calorie intake.

b
Comprehension
Planning
Promotion: Growth and
    Development

11-23. The most effective nutritional counseling intervention for a young pregnant adolescent would be to

a. use one-to-one counseling sessions.

b. use a concrete approach, with the focus on the present rather than the long term.

c. remind her how important her nutrition is to her baby.

d. teach her the recommended daily allowances for important nutrients.

d
Comprehension
Planning
Promotion: Growth and
    Development

11-24. A plan for teaching a postpartum woman about weight loss should include which information?

a. Most women lose about 10 pounds during the first 6 months after delivery.

b. At delivery, a woman usually loses 15-20 pounds.

c. Women who work outside the home have more difficulty losing weight.

d. Weight loss depends, in part, on whether the mother breast-feeds.

a
Application
Analysis/Diagnosis
Promotion: Growth and
    Development

11-25. A woman has come to the clinic for her first postpartum check. After assessing that the client's nutritional status is normal and that she is not breast-feeding her baby, the nurse should advise her to

a. reduce her daily calorie intake by about 300 kcal from her pregnancy intake.

b. continue with the same diet she used during pregnancy.

c. return to prepregnancy levels for all nutrients except protein.

d. see a dietitian for advice on nutrients and calories.

d
Comprehension
Planning
Promotion: Growth and
    Development

11-26. At the first postpartum visit, the nurse should advise a breast-feeding mother to

a. increase her calories by about 500 kcal. over her pregnancy requirements.

b. return to her prepregnancy requirements for protein but not calories.

c. routinely avoid onions, turnips, cabbage and chocolate.

d. keep her calcium intake the same as during pregnancy.

a
Knowledge
Assessment
Promotion: Prevention and
    Early Detection

11-27. If a breast-feeding mother does not have an adequate calorie intake, it is likely that her milk will be

a. reduced in volume.

b. lacking in vitamins.

c. protein deficient.

d. low in calcium.

a
Comprehension
Assessment
Promotion: Growth and
    Development

11-28. Which of the following nutrients is required in the same amount for both pregnant and nonpregnant women?

a. vitamin A

b. vitamin C

c. protein

d. folate

d
Application
Implementation
Physiological:
    Pharmacological and
    Parenteral

11-29. A client in the second trimester of her pregnancy says, "I don't understand why I have to begin iron supplements since I haven't been taking them thus far during pregnancy." Which explanation should the nurse provide?

a. "Actually, we usually do advise iron supplements on the first office visit. Let's ask your doctor about how your case is different."

b. "Iron supplements are not given during the first trimester because iron absorption is higher during that time and the risk of toxicity would be increased."

c. "Iron supplements may not be given during the first trimester because women have adequate iron stores and because iron may increase your fluid retention."

d. "Iron supplements may not be given during the first trimester because the increased demand is still minimal and because iron may increase the woman's nausea."

a

Knowledge

Planning

Promotion: Growth and
  Development

11-30. The protein requirement during pregnancy is about
  a. 10 g/day.
  b. 25 g/day.
  c. 30 g/day.
  d. 60 g/day.

a

Knowledge

Assessment

Promotion: Growth and
  Development

11-31. The ability to achieve good prenatal nutrition is influenced most by
  a. general nutritional status prior to pregnancy.
  b. ability to follow a written diet.
  c. the woman's will power.
  d. the success with which the woman adjusts to pregnancy.

a

Knowledge

Assessment

Promotion: Growth and
  Development

11-32. The greatest amount of maternal weight gain is distributed to the fetus, placenta, and amniotic fluid. What accounts for the second largest amount (5-10 lb.)?
  a. maternal stores
  b. increase in uterine size
  c. increased blood volume
  d. breast tissue

Chapter 12
Pregnancy at Risk: Pregestational Problems

a

Comprehension

Analysis/Diagnosis

Physiological: Reduction of
   Risk Potential

12-1. A type I diabetic is pregnant. When monitoring for complications of pregnancy, it is most important that the nurse assess her

   a. blood pressure.

   b. hemoglobin.

   c. urine output.

   d. lung sounds.

c

Application

Analysis/Diagnosis

Promotion: Prevention and
   Early Detection

12-2. A 26-year-old multipara is 24 weeks pregnant. Her previous births include two large-for-gestational age babies and one unexplained stillbirth. With this history, which of the following assessments should be made in order to identify her most probable pregestational problem? Her

   a. breath sounds.

   b. hemoglobin and hematocrit.

   c. urine and blood glucose.

   d. urine for bacteria.

d

Comprehension

Assessment

Promotion: Prevention and
   Early Detection

12-3. A 26-year-old multipara is 24 weeks pregnant. Her previous births include two large-for-gestational age babies and one unexplained stillbirth. Which of the following tests will most likely be done to definitely determine whether she has gestational diabetes?

   a. a 50 g, 1 hr glucose screening test

   b. a single fasting glucose level

   c. a 100 g, 1 hr glucose tolerance test

   d. a 100 g, 3 hr glucose tolerance test

b

Application

Assessment

Promotion: Prevention and
   Early Detection

12-4. As a part of her routine prenatal care, a client will have a test to screen for gestational diabetes. Therefore, the nurse will need to

   a. perform a finger stick to obtain blood.

   b. collect a voided urine specimen.

   c. have the laboratory technician draw blood from her arm.

   d. tell the client to fast for at least 8 hours before her test.

c

Comprehension

Analysis/Diagnosis

Promotion: Prevention and
Early Detection

12-5. A 28-year-old woman has been an insulin-dependent diabetic for 10 years. She has come to the clinic for a scheduled amniocentesis. She demonstrates understanding of the purpose of the test by stating, "The amniocentesis is done to see if

a. my baby has Down syndrome."

b. my baby is a boy or a girl."

c. my baby is mature enough to be born."

d. I have an intrauterine infection."

a

Application

Analysis/Diagnosis

Promotion: Growth and
Development

12-6. A woman is 34 weeks pregnant. When she comes for an early morning clinic visit she mentions that she did not have time to eat breakfast. Results of her urine specimen show a small amount of ketones to be present in her urine. This most likely indicates

a. pregnancy-induced changes in carbohydrate metabolism.

b. an asymptomatic urinary tract infection.

c. the early onset of gestational diabetes.

d. that her diet is high in fats.

d

Application

Evaluation

Physiological: Reduction of
Risk Potential

12-7. A 21-year-old is 12 weeks pregnant with her first baby. She has cardiac disease, class III, as a result of having had childhood rheumatic fever. During a prenatal visit the nurse reviews the signs of cardiac decompensation with her. The nurse will know that the client understands these signs and symptoms if she states "I would notify my doctor if I have

a. a pulse rate increase of 10 beats per minute."

b. breast tenderness."

c. ankle edema."

d. a frequent cough."

c

Comprehension

Assessment

Physiological: Physiological
Adaptation

12-8. For a pregnant woman with cardiac disease, signs of cardiac decompensation would be especially likely to appear at

a. 12 to 16 weeks' gestation.

b. 20 to 24 weeks' gestation.

c. 28 to 32 weeks' gestation.

d. 36 to 40 weeks' gestation.

12-9. A 21-year-old woman is 12 weeks pregnant with her first baby. She has cardiac disease, class III, as a result of having had childhood rheumatic fever. Which lab result from her initial prenatal visit would alert the nurse to potential problems?

a. urine specific gravity of 1.020

b. hemoglobin of 10 g/dL

c. blood glucose of 80 mg/dL

d. total bilirubin of 0.7 mg/dL

12-10. A client is 12 weeks pregnant with her first baby. She has cardiac disease, class III. She states that she had been taking sodium warfarin (Coumarin), but her physician changed her to heparin. She asks the nurse why this was done. The nurse should reply,

a. "Heparin may be given by mouth while Coumarin must be injected."

b. "Heparin is safer because it does not cross the placenta."

c. "They are the same drug but heparin is less expensive."

d. "Coumarin interferes with iron absorption in the intestines."

12-11. For a pregnant woman, which of the following values indicates anemia?

a. hematocrit of 34 percent

b. hematocrit of 40 percent

c. hemoglobin of 12 g/dL

d. hemoglobin of 9 g/dL

12-12. A pregnant woman is married to an intravenous drug user. She had a negative HIV screening test just after missing her first menstrual period. Which of the following data would indicate that she needs to be retested for HIV?

a. a hemoglobin of 11 g/dL and a rapid weight gain

b. elevated blood pressure and ankle edema

c. shortness of breath and frequent urination

d. unusual fatigue and recurring candida vaginitis

12-13. A client has had a negative test for HIV. Which of the following conclusions is fully justified? She

a. has been infected with the HIV virus.

b. had no HIV antibodies.

c. has not been infected with the HIV virus.

d. will probably develop AIDS.

a

Application

Implementation

Safety: Management of Care

12-14. When assisting with a birth, one of the gloves the nurse is wearing is torn. The nurse should

a. remove the gloves, wash the hands, and apply new gloves.

b. apply a clean glove over the torn one as soon as possible.

c. wait until the delivery is fully accomplished, then wash the hands and apply new gloves.

d. pour hydrogen peroxide over both gloved hands and continue assisting.

b

Knowledge

Analysis/Diagnosis

Physiological: Reduction of Risk Potential

12-15. The fetus of a heroin-addicted mother is likely to

a. be large for gestational age.

b. have meconium aspiration syndrome.

c. be psychologically addicted to heroin.

d. be postmature due to drug-induced relaxation of muscles.

a

Comprehension

Assessment

Promotion: Prevention and Early Detection

12-16. A pregnant woman with a history of heroin addiction should be screened for

a. AIDS.

b. syphilis.

c. asymptomatic bacteremia.

d. tuberculosis.

a

Comprehension

Analysis/Diagnosis

Physiological Physiological Adaptation

12-17. Learning disabilities, decreased interactive behavior, and central nervous system anomalies are frequently found in children whose mothers abused _____ during their pregnancy.

a. cocaine

b. alcohol

c. nicotine

d. marijuana

a

Comprehension

Planning

Promotion: Prevention and Early Detection

12-18. What is the most effective factor in reducing the risk of congenital anomalies in the fetus of a diabetic mother?

a. strict control of blood glucose before conception and in the early weeks of pregnancy

b. continuous monitoring of blood glucose throughout the second and third trimesters

c. careful monitoring for symptoms of retinopathy

d. controlling weight gain to prevent macrosomia

a

Application

Analysis/Diagnosis

Physiological: Reduction of
    Risk Potential

12-19. What do diabetes and iron deficiency anemia have in common? They both increase the chance that the woman will have

a. pregnancy-induced hypertension.

b. monilial vaginitis.

c. hydramnios.

d. postpartal hemorrhage.

a

Application

Assessment

Psychosocial: Coping and
    Adaptation

12-20. A woman's history and appearance suggest drug abuse. The nurse's best approach would be to

a. ask the woman directly, "Do you use any street drugs?"

b. ask the woman if she would like to talk to a counselor.

c. ask some questions about over-the-counter medications before asking about use of illicit drugs.

d. explain how harmful drugs can be for her baby.

c

Comprehension

Analysis/Diagnosis

Promotion: Prevention and
    Early Detection

12-21. Which of the following pregnant women has the greatest risk of developing folic acid deficiency anemia? One

a. who is an African American with no family history of anemias of any kind.

b. who has sickle cell trait or sickle cell anemia.

c. whose diet consists mostly of chips, soft drinks, and "junk food."

d. whose diet is well balanced, except that it is low in iron.

d

Application

Analysis/Diagnosis

Physiological: Reduction of
    Risk Potential

12-22. A 20-year-old woman is at 28 weeks' gestation. Her prenatal history reveals past abuse of drugs, and urine screening indicates that she has recently used heroin. The nurse should recognize that the woman is at increased risk for

a. erythroblastosis fetalis.

b. diabetes mellitus.

c. placenta previa.

d. pregnancy-induced hypertension.

b

Application

Planning

Physiological: Reduction of
    Risk Potential

12-23. A woman is 28 weeks pregnant. She is HIV positive but asymptomatic. Which of the following would be important in managing her pregnancy and delivery?

a. an amniocentesis at 30 and 36 weeks

b. weekly nonstress testing beginning at 32 weeks' gestation

c. application of a fetal scalp electrode as soon as her membranes rupture in labor

d. administration of intravenous antibiotics during labor and delivery

b

Application

Planning

Physiological: Reduction of
Risk Potential

12-24. A 26-year-old multigravida is 24 weeks pregnant. She has developed gestational diabetes. She has a program of regular exercise, which includes walking, bicycling, and swimming. Which of the following instructions should be included in a teaching plan for this client?

a. Exercise either just before meals or wait until 2 hours after a meal.

b. Carry hard candy (or other simple sugar) when exercising.

c. If your fingerstick shows less than 120 mg/dL, ingest 20 g of carbohydrate.

d. If your fingerstick shows more than 120 mg/dL, drink a glass of whole milk or other quick source of carbohydrate.

b

Application

Planning

Physiological: Reduction of
Risk Potential

12-25. A type I, well-controlled, insulin-dependent diabetic is at 20 weeks' gestation. She asks the nurse how her diabetes will affect her baby. The best explanation would include,

a. "Your baby may be smaller than average at birth."

b. "Your baby will probably be larger than average at birth."

c. "As long as you control your blood sugar, your baby will not be affected at all."

d. "There are no effects until about 2 hours after birth, when your baby may have low blood sugar."

a

Comprehension

Analysis/Diagnosis

Physiological: Reduction of
Risk Potential

12-26. A 21-year-old woman is 12 weeks pregnant with her first baby. She has cardiac disease, class III, as a result of having had childhood rheumatic fever. During her pregnancy, which of the following should be her first priority?

a. getting adequate rest

b. taking childbirth education classes

c. restricting travel

d. establishing an exercise program

Chapter 13
Pregnancy at Risk: Gestational Onset

c

Comprehension

Assessment

Promotion: Prevention and
Early Detection

13-1. In order to determine if a client has an ectopic pregnancy, which of the following procedures would be performed?

a. hemoglobin and hematocrit

b. hCG titer

c. pelvic examination

d. amniocentesis

c

Comprehension

Planning

Physiological:
Pharmacological and
Parenteral

13-2. A woman is experiencing preterm labor. To help mature the fetal lungs and decrease the likelihood that her baby will be born with respiratory distress syndrome, the client will be given

a. magnesium sulfate.

b. ritodrine (Yutopar).

c. betamethasone (Celestone).

d. terbutaline (Brethine).

a

Application

Analysis/Diagnosis

Promotion: Prevention and
Early Detection

13-3. A woman has a positive pregnancy test at her first prenatal visit. Her history and physical include the following data. She is gravida 3, para 0; she had a therapeutic abortion with her first 2 pregnancies. She is 40 years old, is slightly anemic, was treated for chlamydia six months ago, and smokes a pack of cigarettes a day. Her partner is unemployed, and they are receiving public assistance. These data indicate that she is statistically at risk for having

a. spontaneous preterm labor.

b. a molar pregnancy.

c. pregnancy induced hypertension.

d. premature rupture of membranes.

b

Comprehension

Analysis/Diagnosis

Physiological: Reduction of
Risk Potential

13-4. A woman has had a dilation and curettage (D&C) because of an incomplete spontaneous abortion. For the week following the D&C, which of the following nursing diagnoses should have the highest priority?

a. grieving

b. risk for infection

c. pain

d. activity intolerance.

13-5. A woman has had her molar pregnancy evacuated and is prepared for discharge. The nurse should make certain that the client understands that it is essential that she

a. not become pregnant for at least one year.

b. receive RhoGAM with her next pregnancy and birth.

c. have her blood pressure checked weekly for the next 30 days.

d. seek genetic counseling with her partner before the next pregnancy.

13-6. During her first prenatal visit to the clinic, a 24-year-old, gravida 1, para 0 client comments, "My blood type is A negative. Will that cause problems with my pregnancy?" The nurse checks the chart and notes that the father's blood type is B positive. The nurse's best response would be,

a. "There is no danger to your baby, but there could be a few minor complications for you. Let's talk about what we can do to prevent those."

b. "We will do a screening test to see if your blood type poses a risk to your baby. If so, we will give you some medication to prevent harm to your baby."

c. "Because your partner is positive and you are negative, there is some risk to the baby; however, we can prevent that by giving you RhoGAM today."

d. "If you were O negative, you might have ABO incompatibility because of your partner's blood type; but since you are type B, there should be no problem."

13-7. The screening test done to determine if a pregnant woman has been sensitized to the Rh factor is the

a. L/S ratio.

b. direct Coombs' test.

c. indirect Coombs' test.

d. maternal bilirubin level.

13-8. A woman's blood type is O negative. Following the birth of her Rh positive baby, she is to receive anti-Rh(D) gamma globulin (RhoGAM). Which of the following nursing actions is CORRECT?

a. Administer the medication subcutaneously.

b. Administer the medication within 72 hours after birth.

c. Administer the medication only if the indirect Coombs' test is positive.

d. Administer the medication only if the infant's blood type is A or B.

b
Comprehension
Analysis/Diagnosis
Promotion: Prevention and
    Early Detection

13-9. A 22-year-old client is expecting her second baby in two weeks. Her blood type is O positive. The nurse might expect blood incompatibility problems if the fetus' blood is

a. Rh negative.

b. type A positive

c. type O negative.

d. any type other than O positive.

a
Application
Planning
Physiological: Physiological
    Adaptation

13-10. A woman in her third trimester of pregnancy is scheduled for open reduction of her fractured radius and ulna. Her postoperative nursing care will include

a. maintaining her in a side-lying position.

b. using minimal narcotics to reduce teratogenic effects.

c. administering oxygen for 24 hours following surgery.

d. providing a bedpan in order to help her maintain bed rest.

c
Application
Implementation
Physiological: Reduction of
    Risk Potential

13-11. A 20-year-old pregnant client's vaginal infection is diagnosed as gonorrhea. Her prenatal history indicates that she has been sexually active since age 15 and has had multiple sexual partners. In teaching her about this disease and its treatment, the nurse should tell her,

a. "Because of this infection, your baby must be born by cesarean birth."

b. "You may want to consider a therapeutic abortion."

c. "All of your sexual partners should be treated if possible."

d. "Gonorrhea can cross the placenta and infect the fetus."

b
Knowledge
Planning
Physiological:
    Pharmacological and
    Parenteral

13-12. Treatment for a pregnant woman with gonorrhea includes the administration of

a. metronidazole (Flagyl).

b. ceftriaxone (Rocephin) and erythromycin (Ilosone).

c. podophyllin (Podofin).

d. benzathine penicillin (Bicillin).

c

Application

Implementation

Promotion: Prevention and
    Early Detection

13-13. A woman is 10 weeks pregnant. Her initial prenatal laboratory screening test for rubella showed an antibody titer of less than 16. The woman calls the clinic and tells the nurse that she has been exposed to measles. The nurse's best response would be,

a. "Since you are in your first trimester of pregnancy, there is not likely to be a problem."

b. "Would you like to see a counselor to talk about your options for the remainder of your pregnancy?"

c. "You should come to the clinic in the next day or two for further evaluation."

d. "You need to have a rubella vaccination immediately. Can you get a ride to the clinic today?"

a

Knowledge

Assessment

Physiological: Physiological
    Adaptation

13-14. A fetus who has been affected by the rubella virus may have

a. permanent hearing loss.

b. spina bifida.

c. cataracts.

d. phocomelia.

d

Application

Planning

Psychosocial: Coping and
    Adaptation

13-15. Laboratory tests indicate that a woman at 10 weeks' gestation has had a recent infection with the rubella virus. Upon medical advice, she decides to have a therapeutic abortion. The nurse's best initial comment to the client should be,

a. "It's for the best. Babies exposed to rubella often have serious birth defects."

b. "It may help you to get pregnant as soon as possible after the abortion."

c. "If you are not comfortable with this, you should see another physician for a second opinion."

d. "I realize this has been a difficult decision for you. How can I help you now?"

b

Comprehension

Assessment

Promotion: Prevention and
    Early Detection

13-16. A client has preeclampsia. She is 33 weeks pregnant and comes to the high-risk screening center for a contraction stress test. In her case, the contraction stress test is being done in order to determine

a. what effect her hypertension has had on the fetus.

b. if the fetus will be able to tolerate labor.

c. if fetal movement increases with contractions.

d. what effect contractions will have on her blood pressure.

b
Application
Analysis/Diagnosis
Physiological: Physiological
    Adaptation

13-17. The nurse has the following data for a woman with preeclampsia Blood pressure 158/100, urinary output 50 mL/hour, lungs clear to auscultation, urine protein 1+ on dipstick, edema of the hands, ankles, and feet. On the next hourly assessment which of the following new data would be a sign that her preeclampsia may be becoming more severe?

a. blood pressure 158/104

b. urinary output 20 mL/hour

c. urine dipstick protein 2+ (kcloves) hint

d. platelet count 110,000

d
Comprehension
Planning
Promotion: Prevention and
    Early Detection

13-18. Which of the following preventive self-care instructions should be included in the teaching plan for a woman who is at high risk for preterm labor?

a. For prenatal breast preparation, use nipple rolling only; do not rub nipples with a towel.

b. Limit fluid intake to 4 glasses of water per day.

c. Rest in bed; get up only to go to the bathroom.

d. Empty your bladder at least every 2 hours while awake.

b
Application
Planning
Physiological: Reduction of
    Risk Potential

13-19. A woman has been admitted to the hospital for severe hyperemesis gravidarum. Which of the following interventions would be needed to prevent complications of severe hyperemesis?

a. Avoid giving very cold or iced liquids.

b. Administer intravenous fluids with potassium chloride added.

c. Have the client rest in bed with her head elevated.

d. Prepare her for an ultrasound to rule out molar pregnancy.

a
Application
Planning
Physiological: Reduction of
    Risk Potential

13-20. A woman is being discharged after being diagnosed with premature rupture of membranes. Which of the following should be included in her discharge teaching?

a. Remain on bed rest, with bathroom privileges.

b. If leaking heavy amounts of fluid, insert a tampon to maintain hygiene.

c. Use a condom if you have intercourse.

d. Contact your physician if you have any further leakage.

d
Comprehension
Analysis/Diagnosis
Promotion: Prevention and
     Early Detection

13-21. Which of the following women is at highest risk for pregnancy-induced hypertension? A/an

a. Caucasian primigravida, age 25.

b. Caucasian multigravida, age 18.

c. African-American multigravida, age 33.

d. African-American primigravida, age 17.

a
Comprehension
Assessment
Physiological: Physiological
     Adaptation

13-22. Why may a client with preeclampsia have an elevated hematocrit?

a. Because her intravascular fluid moves to extracellular spaces due to a decrease in plasma colloid osmotic pressure.

b. Because the need to limit her fluid intake results in a decrease in intravascular fluid volume.

c. Because of the loss of normal vasodilation of the uterine arterioles.

d. Because the high intravascular flow rate damages the endothelium, which in turn causes platelet aggregation.

a
Knowledge
Analysis/Diagnosis
Physiological: Physiological
     Adaptation

13-23. Which of the following findings is indicative of the HELLP syndrome, which sometimes complicates severe preeclampsia?

a. thrombocytopenia

b. edema of the face, hands and feet

c. elevated blood pressure

d. seizures

c
Knowledge
Analysis/Diagnosis
Physiological: Physiological
     Adaptation

13-24. What is the cause of the epigastric pain that sometimes occurs with severe preeclampsia?

a. renal damage

b. increased gastric acidity

c. liver distention

d. internal bleeding

a
Application
Analysis/Diagnosis
Physiological: Physiological
     Adaptation

13-25. A woman is in the first trimester of pregnancy. Her blood pressure is 148/92, she has edema of the hands and feet, and her urine protein is 1+ dipstick. These data are indicative of

a. mild preeclampsia.

b. severe preeclampsia.

c. eclampsia.

d. HELLP syndrome.

c

Comprehension

Planning

Physiological: Physiological
    Adaptation

13-26. A woman is hospitalized with severe preeclampsia. As long as she is able to eat, it is most important that she have a diet that is high in

a. sodium.

b. carbohydrates.

c. protein.

d. magnesium.

b

Application

Analysis/Diagnosis

Physiological: Reduction of
    Risk Potential

13-27. A woman is 30 weeks pregnant. She has come to the hospital because her membranes have ruptured. Based solely on this information, which of the following nursing diagnoses could be made for her (not for the fetus)?

a. risk for impaired gas exchange

b. risk for infection

c. risk for ineffective individual coping

d. risk for fluid volume deficit

b

Application

Analysis/Diagnosis

Physiological: Physiological
    Adaptation

13-28. A baby has just been born by cesarean birth to a mother with active primary herpes (HSV) lesions. The infant has a normal temperature and no symptoms of HSV. The mother says, "I'm so glad he doesn't have herpes. Now I can quit worrying." Which of the following replies conveys accurate information to the mother?

a. "Yes. Because you had a cesarean birth, your baby was not exposed to the virus."

b. "It's a good sign the baby has no symptoms. But we'll need to wait about 2 weeks to be absolutely sure the baby doesn't develop symptoms of herpes."

c. "Yes, it looks good. If your baby's temperature remains normal for the next two days, we'll know for sure that he isn't going to have herpes."

d. "It's good the baby has no symptoms. But I'm sorry to tell you that most babies born to a mother with a primary lesion do develop the disease when they are 2 or 3 days old."

d

Application

Analysis/Diagnosis

Physiological: Reduction of
    Risk Potential

13-29. A 20-year-old woman is at 16 weeks' gestation. She is admitted to the maternity unit with vaginal bleeding and complains of having moderately heavy, brownish vaginal flow. A diagnosis of complete hydatidiform mole is made using ultrasonography. For this client, prior to surgery, it would be most important to monitor frequently the

a. fetal heart tones.

b. oral temperature.

c. urinary output.

d. vaginal bleeding.

b
Comprehension
Analysis/Diagnosis
Physiological: Reduction of
    Risk Potential

13-30. Which of the following nursing diagnoses should have the highest priority for a client with severe hyperemesis gravidarum? Risk for

a. fluid volume deficit.

b. altered nutrition less than body requirements.

c. altered family processes.

d. altered oral mucous membrane.

d
Application
Analysis/Diagnosis
Promotion: Prevention and
    Early Detection

13-31. A 19-year-old woman is expecting her first baby. During the nursing interview, the woman reports that she has been sexually active for 3 years. Two years ago she had gonorrhea, which progressed to pelvic inflammatory disease (PID). Prenatal lab tests show that her hemoglobin value is 11.5 g/dL. Which item from this history data indicates that the client is at risk for an ectopic pregnancy?

a. anemia

b. sexual activity since age 17

c. gonorrhea

d. PID

a
Comprehension
Analysis/Diagnosis
Physiological:
    Pharmacological and
    Parenteral

13-32. A woman is being treated for preterm labor with magnesium sulfate. To be sure to identify early signs of developing drug toxicity, the nurse should check

a. her patellar tendon reflexes.

b. for flushing and a feeling of warmth.

c. her respiratory rate.

d. the fetal heart rate.

b
Application
Planning
Promotion: Prevention and
    Early Detection

13-33. A woman at 30 weeks' gestation is admitted to the emergency department accompanied by her partner. The partner tells the physician that his wife "lost her balance and fell down a flight of stairs." The client is having no vaginal bleeding, uterine contractions, or leaking of amniotic fluid. In addition to assessing the client's vital signs, the emergency nurse should also

a. perform a nitrazine test.

b. monitor the fetal heart rate every 4 hours.

c. check her deep tendon reflexes.

d. check for cervical dilatation.

b

Knowledge

Assessment

Promotion: Prevention and
Early Deteciton

13-34. Which of the following is TRUE regarding the cytomegalovirus?

a. Cytomegalovirus is transmitted through contact with infected cat feces.

b. Cytomegalovirus can be passed transplacentally to the fetus.

c. Cytomegalovirus is the least prevalent of the TORCH group of infections.

d. Cytomegalovirus can be prevented through appropriate vaccination procedures.

Chapter 14
Assessment of Fetal Well-Being

b
Knowledge
Analysis/Diagnosis
Promotion: Prevention and
Early Detection

14-1. Which biophysical profile score would indicate that a fetus is healthy?
a. over 10
b. 8 to 10
c. 4 to 7
d. 0 to 3

b
Knowledge
Assessment
Promotion: Growth and
Development

14-2. Abdominal ultrasound can be used to detect a pregnancy as early as _____ weeks' gestation.
a. 1
b. 6
c. 8
d. 12

b
Knowledge
Assessment
Promotion: Prevention and
Early Detection

14-3. What is the rationale for performing endovaginal rather than transabdominal ultrasound?
a. Endovaginal ultrasound is safer.
b. Endovaginal ultrasound provides a clearer image.
c. Endovaginal ultrasound causes less discomfort.
d. Endovaginal ultrasound can be used later in the pregnancy.

d
Knowledge
Assessment
Promotion: Prevention and
Early Detection

14-4. Ultrasound is especially useful in pregnancy because it
a. causes minimal pain to the mother or fetus.
b. is considered a noninvasive procedure.
c. provides test results within one week.
d. has been found to have no significant fetal risk.

a
Knowledge
Assessment
Promotion: Growth and
Development

14-5. When using ultrasound to determine fetal age during the second trimester, which fetal measurement is most widely used?
a. biparietal diameter
b. crown-rump length
c. total fetal length
d. head-to-abdomen ratio

c
Application
Implementation
Safety: Management of Care

14-6. In assisting with an abdominal ultrasound procedure for determination of fetal age, the nurse

a. asks the woman to sign an informed consent form prior to the procedure.

b. has the woman empty her bladder before the test begins.

c. assists the woman into a supine position on the examining table.

d. instructs the woman to eat a fat-free meal 2 hours before the scheduled test time.

c
Application
Planning
Promotion: Prevention and
    Early Detection

14-7. In preparing a woman for transabdominal chorionic villus sampling, the nurse should

a. place her in the lithotomy position.

b. ask her to empty her bladder.

c. place her in the supine position.

d. cleanse the labia with povidone-iodine (Betadine).

d
Application
Analysis/Diagnosis
Promotion: Prevention and
    Early Detection

14-8. A woman at 28 weeks' gestation is asked to keep a fetal activity diary and bring the results with her to her next clinic visit. One week later she calls the clinic and anxiously tells the nurse that she has not felt the baby move for over 30 minutes. The most appropriate initial comment by the nurse would be,

a. "You need to come to the clinic right away for further evaluation."

b. "Have you been smoking?"

c. "When did you eat last?"

d. "Your baby may be asleep."

a
Application
Evaluation
Promotion: Prevention and
    Early Detection

14-9. At 32 weeks' gestation a woman is scheduled for a second nonstress test (in addition to the one she had at 28 weeks' gestation). Which response by the client would indicate an adequate understanding of this procedure?

a. "I can't get up and walk around during the test."

b. "I'll have an IV started before the test."

c. "I must avoid drinks containing caffeine for 24 hours before the test."

d. "I need to have a full bladder for this test."

c

Application

Analysis/Diagnosis

Promotion: Prevention and
    Early Detection

14-10. During a nonstress test, the nurse notes that the fetal heart rate decelerates about 15 beats during a period of fetal movement. The decelerations occur twice during the test and last 20 seconds each. The nurse realizes these results will be interpreted as

a. a negative test.

b. a reactive test.

c. a nonreactive test.

d. an unsatisfactory test.

c

Application

Planning

Promotion: Prevention and
    Early Detection

14-11. A client who is at 36 weeks' gestation has just had a nonreactive nonstress test. Based on these results, the nurse would prepare the client for

a. a return appointment for an ultrasound examination in 2 weeks.

b. a return appointment for a repeat nonstress test in 1 week.

c. either a contraction stress test or an amniotic fluid index.

d. hospitalization with fetal monitoring.

d

Application

Analysis/Diagnosis

Physiological: Reduction of
    Risk Potential

14-12. A pregnant woman is having a nipple stimulation test. Which of the following results indicates hyperstimulation?

a. the fetal heart rate decelerates when 3 contractions occur within a 10-minute period

b. the fetal heart rate accelerates when contractions last up to 60 seconds

c. there are more than 5 fetal movements in a 10-minute period

d. there are more than 3 uterine contractions in a 6-minute period

d

Application

Analysis/Diagnosis

Promotion: Prevention and
    Early Detection

14-13. During an oxytocin challenge test, the nurse would describe the test as positive if there are

a. no decelerations with 3 contractions in 10 minutes.

b. accelerations of the fetal heart rate with fetal movement.

c. contractions lasting longer than 90 seconds.

d. late decelerations with more than 50 percent of the contractions.

a

Comprehension

Assessment

Safety: Safety and Infection
    Control

14-14. Which of the following actions should the obstetrical nurse take when assisting with amniocentesis?

a. wash her/his hands before donning disposable gloves, and again after removing them

b. force oral fluids to fill the client's bladder

c. encourage the client to lie supine for 15 minutes after the procedure

d. insert a 22-gauge spinal needle into the client's abdomen to withdraw amniotic fluid

c

Application

Analysis/Diagnosis

Physiological: Physiological
    Adaptation

14-15. A physician is considering a cesarean birth because the mother's preeclampsia is worsening. However, the fetus is still premature. Which of the following results would suggest that fetal lungs are mature enough for birth?

a. positive nonstress test

b. a fetal biophysical profile of 8

c. lecithin/sphingomyelin (L/S) ratio of 21

d. absence of phosphatidylglycerol (PG)

a

Application

Evaluation

Physiological: Reduction of
    Risk Potential

14-16. Which response would indicate that a client clearly understands the risks of an amniocentesis?

a. "I might go into labor early."

b. "It could produce a congenital defect in my baby."

c. "Actually, there are no real risks to this procedure."

d. "The test could stunt my baby's growth."

c

Comprehension

Assessment

Promotion: Prevention and
    Early Detection

14-17. A woman at 36 weeks' gestation is having an amniocentesis. Just prior to having the procedure, she has an ultrasound done. The purpose of an ultrasound at that time is to

a. determine if there is more than one fetus.

b. prescreen the fetus for gross congenital anomalies.

c. locate the placenta and fetus.

d. estimate the fetal age.

c

Application

Implementation

Promotion: Prevention and
    Early Detection

14-18. A client is having an amniocentesis. She asks the nurse if the procedure will hurt. The nurse should respond

a. "There will be very little discomfort."

b. "You will have an epidural anesthetic so you won't feel anything."

c. "There will be some discomfort when the needle is inserted into your abdomen."

d. "Would you like to talk to other women who have had this procedure?"

a

Comprehension

Implementation

Physiological: Reduction of
  Risk Potential

14-19. The nurse prepares a pregnant woman for amniocentesis by

a. making sure the woman has signed her consent form
before the procedure.

b. starting an intravenous infusion just before the procedure.

c. administering oxygen with a non-rebreathing face mask.

d. having her assume a comfortable position on her left side.

d

Application

Analysis/Diagnosis

Promotion: Prevention and
  Early Detection

14-20. Which of the following test results on the amniotic fluid
would indicate that the fetus is at least 36 weeks' gestation?

a. a creatinine level of 2.1 mg/dL

b. 8 percent of the fetal fat cells stained orange with Nile blue
sulfate

c. a small amount of meconium is present

d. the presence of phosphatidylglycerol (PG) in the fluid

a

Comprehension

Assessment

Promotion: Prevention and
  Early Detection

14-21. What is the purpose of Doppler velocimetry? To

a. assess placental function by studying blood flow changes.

b. diagnose and treat fetal cardiac arrhythmias prior to birth.

c. determine whether the fetal nervous system is intact.

d. provide a piece of information for the fetal biophysical
profile.

c

Application

Analysis/Diagnosis

Promotion: Prevention and
  Early Detection

14-22. Compared to a standard *nonstress test*, one advantage of a
fetal acoustic stimulation test (FAST) as an adjunct is that the
FAST

a. is a noninvasive technique.

b. is easy to perform.

c. takes less time to obtain results.

d. tests for fetal well-being.

d

Comprehension

Analysis/Diagnosis

Physiological: Reduction of
  Risk Potential

14-23. Which of the following women would be a candidate for a
contraction stress test (CST)? One who

a. has unexplained vaginal bleeding in the third trimester.

b. has had premature rupture of the membranes.

c. is carrying triplets.

d. is carrying a fetus with intrauterine growth retardation.

a

Application

Assessment

Promotion: Prevention and
    Early Detection

14-24. A couple has a 5-year-old child with Down syndrome. The woman has a positive pregnancy test, and is about 10 weeks pregnant. They have decided to have an abortion if this fetus has Down syndrome. Therefore, the most important/useful antenatal test for them to have would be

a. chorionic villus sampling.

b. amniocentesis with AFP (alpha-fetoprotein) screening.

c. magnetic resonance imaging (MRI).

d. percutaneous umbilical blood sampling.

b

Comprehension

Analysis/Diagnosis

Promotion: Prevention and
    Early Detection

14-25. A woman is at 32 weeks' gestation. Her fundal height measurement at this clinic appointment is 26 centimeters. After reviewing her ultrasound results, the health care provider asks the nurse to schedule the client for a series of sonograms to be done every 2 weeks. The nurse should make sure that the client understands that the main purpose for this is to

a. assess for congenital anomalies.

b. evaluate fetal growth.

c. grade the placenta.

d. rule out a suspected hydatidiform mole.

a

Application

Analysis/Diagnosis

Physiological: Reduction of
    Risk Potential

14-26. A 28-year-old woman has been an insulin-dependent diabetic for 10 years. At 36 weeks' gestation she has an amniocentesis. A lecithin/sphingomyelin (L/S) ratio test is performed on the sample of her amniotic fluid. Since she is a diabetic, the 2:1 ratio obtained indicates that the fetus

a. has a low risk of RDS.

b. has an intrauterine infection.

c. has a neural tube defect.

d. is at risk for hyperglycemia.

Chapter 15
Processes and Stages of Labor and Birth

c

Comprehension

Assessment

Promotion: Growth and
Development

15-1. Which of the following factors have a positive influence on a woman's perception of her birth experience?

a. maternal age under 35 years

b. having had a previous child

c. support from a partner during labor

d. middle or upper socioeconomic status

c

Application

Analysis/Diagnosis

Promotion: Growth and
Development

15-2. What is the similarity between the anterior fontanelle and the posterior fontanelle of a newborn? Both

a. measure about 2 x 3 cm.

b. close at about 18 months.

c. are the intersections of the cranial sutures.

d. are used in labor to identify station.

c

Comprehension

Analysis/Diagnosis

Promotion: Growth and
Development

15-3. It is good to have a vertex presentation with the fetal head flexed chin-to-chest because this position

a. keeps the cord from prolapsing when the woman sits up.

b. allows the occipitofrontal diameter of the head to present to the maternal pelvis.

c. allows the smallest diameter of the head to present to the maternal pelvis.

d. allows the fetal head to hyperextend as it enters the birth canal.

a

Knowledge

Analysis/Diagnosis

Promotion: Growth and
Development

15-4. Which of the following is considered to be an "abnormal" presentation (a malpresentation)?

a. shoulder

b. military

c. face

d. vertex

c

Comprehension

Assessment

Promotion: Growth and
Development

15-5. In normal labor, as the uterine contractions become stronger, they usually also become

a. less frequent.

b. less painful.

c. longer in duration.

d. shorter in duration.

b
Application
Implementation
Promotion: Growth and
    Development

15-6. Four minutes after the birth of a client's baby, there is a sudden gush of blood from her vagina and about 8 inches of umbilical cord slides out of her vagina. What should the nurse do?

    a. Place the bed in Trendelenberg position.

    b. Watch for the emergence of the placenta.

    c. Give IV oxytocin to stop the bleeding.

    d. Roll her onto her left side.

b
Comprehension
Assessment
Promotion: Growth and
    Development

15-7. When performing a vaginal examination during labor, the nurse feels the presenting part at 1 centimeter below the woman's ischial spines. The nurse should chart the station as

    a. -1.

    b. +1.

    c. floating.

    d. engaged.

c
Application
Analysis/Diagnosis
Promotion: Growth and
    Development

15-8. A nurse wishes to evaluate the progress of a woman's labor. The nurse obtains the following data: Cervical dilatation 2 cm; contractions mild, occurring every 2 minutes, and duration 30-40 seconds. Which cue in the preceding data does NOT fit the patterns suggested by the rest of the cues?

    a. cervical dilatation 2 cm

    b. contraction intensity mild

    c. contraction frequency every 2 minutes

    d. contraction duration 30-40 seconds

c
Knowledge
Assessment
Promotion: Prevention and
    Early Detection

15-9. The duration of a uterine contraction is measured from the

    a. beginning of one contraction to the beginning of another contraction.

    b. end of one contraction to the beginning of the next contraction.

    c. beginning of one contraction until the end of the same contraction.

    d. end of one contraction to the end of the next contraction.

b
Comprehension
Assessment
Promotion: Growth and
    Development

15-10. A client says, "I'm not sure this is it. I have had one episode of false labor before." When assessing to see if the woman is in true labor, the nurse will look for

    a. any evidence of bloody show.

    b. progressive effacement and dilation of the cervix.

    c. the client's report that she had a sudden burst of energy.

    d. contraction and relaxation of the uterus.

b
Application
Assessment
Promotion: Growth and
  Development

15-11. A woman believes she is in labor. The nurse asks how frequently her contractions have been coming. Her partner gives the nurse a paper with the following times 12:05 a.m., 12:10 a.m., 12:15 a.m., 12:20 a.m. He tells the nurse that each of these times marks the beginning of a contraction. From these times, the nurse can calculate that

a. there is no useful information about the contractions.

b. the frequency of contractions is every 5 minutes.

c. the duration of contractions is 5 minutes.

d. the client's contractions are increasing in intensity.

d
Application
Assessment
Promotion: Growth and
  Development

15-12. A laboring woman states that her contractions feel "pretty strong." The nurse assesses the next three contractions and her fingers are unable to indent the uterine wall. The nurse would chart the intensity of these contractions as

a. slight.

b. mild.

c. moderate.

d. strong.

b
Knowledge
Assessment
Promotion: Growth and
  Development

15-13. "Presentation" refers to the

a. relationship of the presenting part to the mother's pelvis.

b. part of the fetal body first entering the mother's pelvis.

c. flexion and extension of the fetal body and extremities.

d. relationship of the cephalocaudal axis of the fetus to the maternal spine.

c
Knowledge
Assessment
Promotion: Growth and
  Development

15-14. The type of maternal pelvis most favorable for a vaginal birth is

a. polypoid.

b. android.

c. gynecoid.

d. platypelloid.

a
Comprehension
Analysis/Diagnosis
Promotion: Growth and
  Development

15-15. The birthing nurse performs a vaginal examination and determines that the biparietal diameter of the fetal head has reached the pelvic inlet. The nurse will chart that the fetus is

a. engaged.

b. at the level of the ischial spines.

c. floating.

d. at zero station.

b
Application
Implementation
Promotion: Growth and
    Development

15-16. A woman asks the nurse, "Do you think I will have an easy labor?" The nurse's best response would be,

a. "There is no way to know how your labor will proceed. Everyone is different."

b. "There are several interrelated factors that determine the length and difficulty of your labor."

c. "Well, labor is never really easy. Labor means hard work."

d. "It is too soon to tell, but we have lots of pain relief measures if it gets too bad."

c
Knowledge
Assessment
Promotion: Growth and
    Development

15-17. The mechanism of labor that allows the fetal head to present itself to fit the widest anteroposterior diameter of the pelvic cavity is

a. descent.

b. flexion.

c. internal rotation.

d. extension.

c
Knowledge
Assessment
Promotion: Growth and
    Development

15-18. The most intense portion of the uterine contraction is termed the

a. increment.

b. decrement.

c. acme.

d. nadir.

d
Knowledge
Assessment
Promotion: Growth and
    Development

15-19. The hormone that inhibits the development of uterine contractions during pregnancy is

a. estrogen.

b. oxytocin.

c. prostaglandin.

d. progesterone.

d
Application
Implementation
Promotion: Growth and
    Development

15-20. A woman in the first stage of labor asks, "If it is my cervix that is stretching and opening, why do I have pain in my back?" The nurse explains that the primary reason for the additional discomfort is

a. distention of the vagina.

b. pressure of the presenting part on the floor of the perineum.

c. muscle tension in the arms, legs, and hips.

d. referred pain from the uterus.

d
Application
Analysis/Diagnosis
Promotion: Growth and
    Development

15-21. A laboring primigravida complains of increasing rectal pressure. A vaginal examination reveals a cervix that is 8 centimeters dilated and 100 percent effaced. The fetal head is at +2 station. The nurse can correctly conclude that the

a. woman may start to push with the next contraction.

b. woman should deliver within the next 30 minutes.

c. baby is very high and the woman will need to do a lot of pushing.

d. fetus has descended well down into the birth canal.

c
Application
Analysis/Diagnosis
Promotion: Growth and
    Development

15-22. A 19-year-old Mexican-American woman is in labor. Her cervix is 8 centimeters dilated and 100 percent effaced. The fetal head is at +2 station. She is beginning to feel rectal pressure, and is showing signs of irritability and restlessness. She says, "I can't take this any more." The nurse should explain to the client that her behavior is

a. likely, if it continues, to interfere with the progress of her labor.

b. unexpected for a married woman of her cultural background.

c. understandable and is to be expected at this phase of the labor process.

d. frightening the other clients and she should try to regain control.

c
Knowledge
Assessment
Promotion: Growth and
    Development

15-23. The process of taking up the cervical canal by the uterine walls and changing it into a paper-thin circular structure is known as

a. engagement.

b. ripening.

c. effacement.

d. dilation.

a
Comprehension
Implementation
Promotion: Growth and
    Development

15-24. The client observes the vaginal birth of her first child by looking in the mirror. She says that after the birth of the baby's head, with the face looking at the floor, the baby turned its head to the right on its own, without being touched. The nurse tells the client that this is a normal mechanism called

a. external rotation.

b. flexion.

c. extension.

d. internal rotation.

d
Comprehension
Assessment
Promotion: Growth and
    Development

15-25. A primigravida client tells the nurse that about 2 weeks before going into labor she noticed her breathing became easier, but she had to go to the bathroom more frequently. What the client experienced is commonly called

a. quickening.

b. dilation.

c. dropping.

d. lightening.

c
Application
Planning
Promotion: Growth and
    Development

15-26. A client telephones to say that she has had some bloody show and may have lost her mucous plug. She says she needs to urinate more frequently, and is having some leg cramps. One thing the nurse should tell her is

a. to come to the office to be evaluated right away.

b. to limit her fluids at bedtime, and lie down when she has leg cramps.

c. that her labor will probably begin within the next 24-48 hours.

d. that her symptoms are normal and she does not need to call unless her water breaks.

a
Knowledge
Assessment
Promotion: Growth and
    Development

15-27. One of the signs of impending labor is

a. a sudden weight loss of 1-3 lb.

b. increasing fatigue.

c. shortness of breath.

d. increased fetal movements.

c
Application
Analysis/Diagnosis
Promotion: Growth and
    Development

15-28. A laboring client is having contractions every 2 to 3 minutes, lasting 60 to 90 seconds, and of strong intensity. The fetal head is visualized when the client pushes involuntarily. A vaginal examination reveals a completely dilated and effaced cervix. What stage of labor is the client in?

a. transition

b. third

c. second

d. active

d
Application
Implementation
Promotion: Growth and
    Development

15-29. The client, who is in transitional labor, screams, "Leave me alone!" The nurse should

a. ask another nurse to stay with the client.

b. ask the client why she wants to be left alone.

c. notify the physician immediately.

d. remain with the client.

c

Comprehension

Assessment

Promotion: Growth and
Development

15-30. Which of the following fetal responses is thought to be caused by compression of the fetal head during transition and second stage?

a. an increase in blood pH

b. cessation of fetal breathing movements

c. early decelerations of the fetal heart rate

d. a drop in fetal oxygen saturation

a

Comprehension

Assessment

Promotion: Prevention and
Early Detection

15-31. Which of the following must be measured with an *intrauterine catheter* and fetal monitor in order to be accurate?

a. intensity of uterine contractions

b. duration of uterine contractions

c. frequency of uterine contractions

d. fetal heart rate accelerations

c

Application

Analysis/Diagnosis

Promotion: Prevention and
Early Detection

15-32. The client has given birth to a healthy infant and is now being taken to the recovery room. The *priority maternal* assessment the nurse should make in the first 2 hours after birth is for

a. nausea and vomiting.

b. urinary retention.

c. hemodynamic changes.

d. temperature elevation.

Chapter 16
Intrapartal Nursing Assessment

c

Application

Analysis/Diagnosis

Promotion: Growth and
    Development

16-1. When performing an intrapartal assessment during the first stage of labor, which of the following findings should the nurse report to the nurse-midwife?

a. clear, blood-tinged mucus from the vagina

b. fetal heart rate of 146 bpm

c. cervical edema with failure to efface

d. woman wishes to wear her own clothes

c

Comprehension

Analysis/Diagnosis

Promotion: Prevention and
    Early Detection

16-2. Repetitive variable decelerations in fetal heart rate should lead you to suspect

a. impending second stage labor.

b. compression of the fetal head.

c. occult umbilical cord prolapse or nuchal cord.

d. a breech presentation of the baby.

b

Application

Assessment

Promotion: Growth and
    Development

16-3. A client in labor tells the nurse that she thinks her water has broken. Which of the following tests will the nurse perform to confirm?

a. shake test

b. nitrazine test

c. dextrostix test

d. urinalysis

   Answer: 69

d

Knowledge

Assessment

Promotion: Growth and
    Development

16-4. During the initial intrapartal assessment of a client in early labor, the nurse performs a vaginal examination to obtain information about the

a. uterine contraction pattern.

b. fetal position.

c. presence of the mucous plug.

d. cervical dilation and effacement.

a

Application

Implementation

Safety: Safety and Infection
    Control

16-5. Sterile gloves should be worn when the nurse

a. places fetal scalp electrodes.

b. helps the client remove clothing that is damp with amniotic fluid.

c. changes wet bedding.

d. handles lab tubes filled with fetal blood.

a
Comprehension
Assessment
Promotion: Prevention and
    Early Detection

16-6. A woman is admitted to the birthing suite. After determining that she is in early labor and obtaining a brief history, the nurse should *next*

a. check for intrapartal risk factors.

b. perform the intrapartal physical assessment.

c. perform a psychosocial-cultural assessment.

d. check the client's cervix for dilation and effacement.

b
Knowledge
Assessment
Promotion: Growth and
    Development

16-7. The nurse determines fetal presentation and position by performing Leopold's maneuvers. The second maneuver in this procedure is used to determine

a. whether the fetal head or buttocks occupies the uterine fundus.

b. the location of the fetal back.

c. whether the head or buttocks lies in the pelvic inlet.

d. the descent of the presenting part into the pelvis.

d
Application
Assessment
Promotion: Prevention and
    Early Detection

16-8. The nurse is preparing to assess the fetal heart rate (FHR) and has determined that the fetal back is located toward the client's left side, the small part toward the right side, and that there is a vertex presentation. The nurse should initially begin auscultating the heart rate in the mother's

a. right upper quadrant.

b. right lower quadrant.

c. left upper quadrant.

d. left lower quadrant.

a
Application
Analysis/Diagnosis
Promotion: Growth and
    Development

16-9. The nurse obtains a fetal heart rate (FHR) of 144 beats per minute (BPM). The nurse will interpret this rate as being

a. normal.

b. too slow.

c. a little too fast, bears watching.

d. dangerously fast.

c
Application
Planning
Promotion: Growth and
    Development

16-10. A woman is admitted to the birthing suite in early labor. She and her partner have completed a childbirth preparation course. The nurse obtains an initial FHR of 128 beats per minute, and decides not to initiate external electronic fetal monitoring at this time because external monitoring would

a. not allow her to detect normal baseline changes.

b. be too distracting for the couple.

c. restrict the woman's movement.

d. not be accurate in this situation.

b
Application
Analysis/Diagnosis
Promotion: Growth and
    Development

16-11. A woman is in active labor. Her cervical dilation is 6 cm. The nurse notes that the fetal heart rate (FHR) slows from its baseline of 144 beats per minute (BPM) to 126 BPM from the acme of the contraction. The FHR then returns to its baseline by the end of the contraction. The nurse understands that this indicates

a. fetal hypoxia.

b. fetal head compression.

c. deterioration of the placental unit.

d. maternal hypoxia.

d
Application
Assessment
Promotion: Prevention and
    Early Detection

16-12. Assessment of a laboring client reveals that her cervix is 10 centimeters dilated and she is pushing. The nurse should begin checking the fetal heart rate

a. for a full minute.

b. during each contraction.

c. every 5 minutes.

d. immediately after each contraction.

a
Application
Assessment
Promotion: Prevention and
    Early Detection

16-13. A 32-year-old gravida 2 comes to the birthing area in active labor. She is diabetic. During the admission interview, she tells the nurse that she gave birth to a stillborn infant 2 years ago. The nurse initiates indirect (external) fetal heart rate monitoring. In this situation, the best device for this procedure is the

a. transducer.

b. fetal scalp electrode.

c. fetoscope.

d. ultrasound stethoscope.

c
Comprehension
Assessment
Promotion: Prevention and
    Early Detection

16-14. The rationale for using direct (internal) fetal heart rate monitoring is

a. direct monitoring can be used throughout the birth process.

b. indirect monitoring is subject to artifacts.

c. direct monitoring provides more accurate data than external monitoring.

d. indirect monitoring cannot be used until the cervix is dilated to 2 centimeters.

c

Application

Analysis/Diagnosis

Physiological: Reduction of
  Risk Potential

16-15. A woman is in labor. The fetus is in vertex position. Her membranes rupture and the amniotic fluid is meconium stained. The nurse performs a vaginal examination to determine cervical status and check the internal fetal electrode; but primarily, the nurse is assessing for

a. fetal descent.

b. fetal position change.

c. prolapsed umbilical cord.

d. caput succedaneum.

c

Application

Analysis/Diagnosis

Promotion: Prevention and
  Early Detection

16-16. The nurse notices that a fetal heart rate begins to decline from its baseline of 144 beats per minute (BPM) to 110 BPM after the acme of each contraction. The wave is uniform, with a shape reflecting the contraction. The nurse recognizes this deviation as

a. fetal bradycardia.

b. early deceleration.

c. late deceleration.

d. variable deceleration.

a

Knowledge

Analysis/Diagnosis

Promotion: Growth and
  Development

16-17. Which of the following would be interpreted as a reassuring fetal heart rate pattern?

a. early decelerations

b. a sinusoidal pattern

c. variable decelerations with little variability

d. intermittent late decelerations with good variability

b

Application

Implementation

Promotion: Prevention and
  Detection

16-18. The nurse documents client data on the fetal monitor strip. Which of the following entries is the most useful, specific, and complete?

a. amniotomy with clear fluid; vaginal examination performed

b. spontaneous rupture of membranes with meconium-stained fluid; cervix 8 cm dilated and 100 percent effaced

c. spontaneous rupture of membranes; vaginal examination done; oxygen administered

d. artificial rupture of membranes; scalp electrode applied; linens changed

a

Application

Implementation

Physiological: Physiological
    Adaption

16-19. A woman's membranes have ruptured spontaneously. The fluid is meconium stained. After applying an internal electrode, the nurse sees that the client is having late decelerations. The nurse's next action should be to

a. turn the client to her left side.

b. monitor the client's blood pressure.

c. administer oxygen by nasal cannula.

d. assess the client's hydration status.

d

Application

Implementation

Physiological: Reduction of
    Risk Potential

16-20. A client's membranes have ruptured spontaneously. The fluid is meconium stained. After an internal electrode is applied, she asks why she needs to have the internal fetal monitoring. The nurse's best response would be to

a. reassure the client that her baby is fine.

b. refer the question to her physician.

c. tell the client that release of meconium indicates fetal distress.

d. explain that the meconium means that the baby needs to be observed more closely.

b

Knowledge

Analysis/Diagnosis

Physiological: Reduction of
    Risk Potential

16-21. Which of the following fetal blood pH results indicates severe depression of the fetus?

a. 7.2 or less

b. 7.3 or less

c. 7.3 or more

d. 7.4 or more

c

Application

Implementation

Physiological: Reduction of
    Risk Potential

16-22. After noting meconium-stained amniotic fluid, fetal heart rate decelerations, and unsatisfactory fetal blood pH results, the physician diagnoses a severely depressed fetus. The appropriate nursing action at this time would be to

a. increase the oxygen being administered to the mother.

b. change the mother's position to left lateral.

c. prepare the mother for a forceps or cesarean birth.

d. start an intravenous infusion of 1/4 normal saline.

c

Application

Implementation

Promotion: Prevention and
Early Detection

16-23. A laboring primigravida has had an external monitor applied. The nurse periodically places her hand on the client's fundus during the contractions. The client asks if everything is all right. The nurse should reply,

a. "I need to make sure that the machine is working properly."

b. "Sometimes the monitors don't give accurate readings so I double check."

c. "Palpating a few of your contractions gives me a better idea of how strong they really are."

d. "I would rather do this the old-fashioned way and not rely completely on technology."

d

Comprehension

Assessment

Promotion: Prevention and
Early Detection

16-24. A laboring primigravida has had an external fetal monitor applied. The nurse periodically examines the monitor tracing. The client asks why this is necessary when the heart rate is normal. Which statement best explains the nurse's behavior?

a. "The fetal heart rate tracing is a legal document that must be checked for accuracy."

b. "Examination of the fetal heart rate tracing can help predict the fetal outcome."

c. "The fetal monitor records data, but the nurse must interpret the information."

d. "A fetus that is in distress may have a normal heart rate but have other subtle changes that will show up as a pattern on the strip."

d

Knowledge

Assessment

Promotion: Prevention and
Early Detection

16-25. Which of the following is a change in the baseline fetal heart rate?

a. acceleration

b. late deceleration

c. sinusoidal pattern

d. tachycardia

d

Comprehension

Assessment

Promotion: Prevention and
Early Detection

16-26. A woman is in labor. Her contractions are *not* being electronically monitored. In order to best assess the uterine contractions, the nurse should

a. palpate just above the symphysis pubis.

b. ask the woman about her contractions.

c. observe the woman's behavior and facial expression.

d. palpate the uterine fundus.

d
Application
Implementation
Physiological

16-27. A woman is in labor. The fetus is in vertex position. When the client's membranes rupture, the nurse sees that the amniotic fluid is meconium stained. The nurse should immediately

a. change the client's position in bed.

b. notify the physician that birth is imminent.

c. administer oxygen at 2 liters per minute.

d. begin continuous fetal heart rate monitoring.

b
Application
Analysis/Diagnosis
Promotion: Growth and
   Development

16-28. The external monitor shows a fetal heart rate of 140 with decreased long-term variability and absent short-term variability. The nurse should

a. turn the woman to her left side.

b. obtain a medical order for an internal monitor.

c. increase the intravenous flow rate.

d. recognize an emergency and page the physician.

c
Application
Implementation
Promotion: Growth and
   Development

16-29. When a client's membranes rupture during labor, the nurse should *first*

a. change the perineal pad.

b. chart the appearance of the fluid.

c. check the fetal heart rate.

d. position the woman on her left side.

Chapter 17
The Family in Childbirth: Needs and Care

d
Comprehension
Planning
Safe Environment:
    Management of Care

17-1. For which of the following women might it be especially important to offer warm water instead of ice chips or cold water during the birth experience? A woman of _____ culture

a. African American

b. Eastern European

c. Latino

d. Laotian

b
Application
Analysis/Diagnosis
Promotion: Growth and
    Development

17-2. The nurse observes that a woman in the latent phase of labor is grimacing during contractions. The woman, a primigravida, says the contractions feel like menstrual cramps and that she is glad to be in labor. The nurse assesses this information as

a. being incongruent.

b. expected during this phase of labor.

c. inappropriate for a primigravida.

d. euphoria.

a
Application
Analysis/Diagnosis
Promotion: Growth and
    Development

17-3. A client is having mild uterine contractions, about 20 minutes apart, lasting 30 seconds. She grimaces during contractions, but reports that she is glad to be in labor and that the contractions feel like menstrual cramps. On the basis of this data, the most appropriate nursing diagnosis would be

a. risk for pain.

b. ineffective individual coping.

c. knowledge deficit.

d. anxiety.

c
Application
Planning
Promotion: Growth and
    Development

17-4. A woman is brought to the hospital in active labor by her partner. She is brought by wheelchair to the birthing area and greeted by the nurse. What is the nurse's *first priority* in admitting the woman?

a. determine the couple's goals for the birth experience

b. assess the woman's coping mechanisms

c. assess the imminence of birth

d. determine the presence or absence of a support system

a

Comprehension

Assessment

Promotion: Growth and
Development

17-5. By inquiring about a laboring woman's expectations for her labor and birth, the nurse is *primarily*

a. recognizing the client as an active participant in her own care.

b. attempting to correct any misinformation the client may have received.

c. acting as an advocate for the client.

d. establishing rapport with the client.

b

Comprehension

Planning

Promotion: Growth and
Development

17-6. A woman is in latent labor. Her membranes are intact; her contractions are mild. Considering the woman's condition and phase of labor, the nurse should anticipate that the woman's activity orders will be

a. complete bed rest.

b. ambulation ad lib.

c. bathroom privileges.

d. up in chair t.id. .

c

Comprehension

Planning

Promotion: Growth and
Development

17-7. The nurse can best utilize the period of latent labor for

a. teaching the client about newborn care.

b. dispelling myths about childbirth.

c. teaching breathing techniques for use during labor.

d. allowing the client to rest as much as possible.

b

Application

Assessment

Promotion: Growth and
Development

17-8. During admission of a multipara, the nurse assesses that contractions are occurring every 3 minutes and lasting 45 seconds. The client says she has been in labor for approximately 10 hours. It is *most* important at this time for the nurse to assess the

a. time the client last ate.

b. cervical dilation.

c. allergies to medications.

d. oral temperature.

c

Comprehension

Analysis

Psychosocial: Coping and
Adaptation

17-9. During each of the vaginal examinations, a laboring woman continually tries to pull her hospital gown down to cover her perineum. The nurse understands that the client's behavior reflects her

a. lack of understanding of hospital procedures.

b. attempt to keep warm.

c. attempt to preserve her modesty.

d. noncompliance with the treatment plan.

a
Application
Planning
Promotion: Growth and
    Development

17-10. The client's contractions are occurring every 2 to 3 minutes, lasting 90 seconds, and are very strong. She complains of back pain. A vaginal examination reveals cervical dilation of 9 cm and a +2 station. The nurse can best promote comfort during this phase by

a. applying firm pressure to the woman's sacrum.

b. washing the woman's perineum.

c. encouraging the woman to void.

d. placing a cool cloth behind the woman's neck.

d
Knowledge
Analysis
Physiological: Adaptation

17-11. During transition, the client complains of tingling in her fingers and around her mouth. The nurses recognizes these as clinical manifestations of

a. hypercapnia.

b. anxiety.

c. imminent birth.

d. hyperventilation.

b
Application
Implementation
Physiological: Reduction of
    Risk Potential

17-12. A woman in labor has begun to complain of numbness in her lips and fingers. She says she feels dizzy and is seeing spots. The nurse should

a. notify the physician immediately.

b. count out loud to help her slow her breathing.

c. take the client's blood pressure

d. turn the client to her left side.

a
Application
Implementation
Promotion: Growth and
    Development

17-13. A laboring woman feels the urge to push, but her cervix is not fully dilated. The nurse can best help the client by

a. helping her control the sensation by coaching her to use third level (hee hee hoo) breathing.

b. explaining that pushing will make her cervix edematous and prolong her labor.

c. telling her to hold her breath and push gently for 5 seconds at a time.

d. performing urinary catheterization to empty the client's bladder.

c
Comprehension
Planning
Promotion: Growth and
    Development

17-14. At birth of the infant, the nursing intervention that promotes the nursing goal of parental attachment is

a. allowing the mother to rest immediately after delivering.

b. transferring the infant to the newborn nursery for its initial assessment.

c. positioning the baby on the mother's chest.

d. placing the infant in the warmer, facing the mother.

b
Comprehension
Evaluation
Physiological:
    Pharmacological and
    Parenteral

17-15. A client's physician has ordered an oxytocic drug to be given after the birth of an infant. The nurse knows that if this drug is effective the client will have

a. decreased discomfort.

b. a contracted uterus.

c. a soft uterus.

d. decreased blood pressure.

a
Comprehension
Plan
Promotion: Growth and
    Development

17-16. Which of the following should be included in the nursing care of a client during the fourth stage of labor?

a. assessing for vaginal bleeding every 15 minutes

b. continuous massage of the uterine fundus

c. assisting the mother to use the sitz bath

d. administering a small Fleets-type enema

c
Application
Assessment
Promotion: Growth and
    Development

17-17. A client has given birth to a baby. The infant's heart rate is 100 beats per minute and he is crying vigorously. His limbs are flexed, his trunk is pink, and his hands and feet are cyanotic. The infant cries when the soles of his feet are stimulated. Based on these findings, the Apgar score for this infant would be

a. 7.

b. 8.

c. 9.

d. 10.

b
Knowledge
Assessment
Promotion: Prevention and
    Early Detection

17-18. An infant's Apgar score is ascertained after birth at 1 minute and again at _____ minutes.

a. 2

b. 5

c. 10

d. 15

b
Comprehension
Planning
Promotion: Growth and
    Development

17-19. The *first* priority in caring for the newborn immediately after birth is

a. maintenance of warmth.

b. maintenance of respirations.

c. identification of the newborn.

d. promotion of attachment.

d
Comprehension
Planning
Promotion: Growth and
    Devleopment

17-20. Immediately after birth, the nurse has established that the infant's respirations are satisfactory. The nurse's next priority is to

a. suction the baby with a bulb syringe.

b. calculate the Apgar score.

c. collect cord blood for banking.

d. dry the baby's head and body well.

d
Comprehension
Assessment
Psychosocial: Coping and
    Adaptation

17-21. Compared to the admission considerations for an adult woman in labor, the nurse's *priority* assessment for an adolescent in labor should consider the client's

a. cultural background.

b. plans to keep the infant.

c. support person.

d. developmental level.

b
Application
Planning
Promotion: Growth and
    Development

17-22. A woman has given birth prior to the arrival of the physician. In this situation, which of the following nursing actions is *most* appropriate to decrease postpartal bleeding?

a. administering 10 units of Pitocin IM

b. putting the infant to breast

c. continuously massaging the fundus

d. inserting a perineal pad in the vagina

b
Application
Implementation
Promotion: Growth and
    Development

17-23. A woman telephones the birthing unit to say that she has been having regular uterine contractions, 15 minutes apart for 2 hours. She says that she does *not* think her water has broken and that this is her first baby. After assessing to confirm that the membranes are indeed intact, what should the nurse tell her?

a. To come to the birth setting to be evaluated to see if she is in true labor.

b. To come to the birth setting when the contractions are 5 minutes apart, or when her water breaks.

c. To lie down, not eat any solid foods, and call back if the pain does not go away in an hour or two.

d. To call her physician to see if he wants to see her in his office today.

a
Comprehension
Assessment
Promotion: Growth and
    Development

17-24. During the admission interview a woman states that she has had some episodes of spotting of blood during the last month, but with no pain. Which of the following assessments is *contraindicated*?

a. sterile vaginal examination

b. urinalysis

c. palpation of uterine contractions

d. fetal monitoring by Doppler

c
Application
Analysis
Promotion: Growth and
    Development

17-25. A woman is using breathing techniques during active labor. Which of the following assessments indicates that the nurse needs to help her with her breathing? The woman

a. says that her mouth is dry.

b. is perspiring.

c. says that her fingers feel numb.

d. sleeps between contractions.

a
Application
Analysis
Physiological: Basic Care and
    Comfort

17-26. The Lamaze method uses three levels of chest breathing. What do those three techniques have in common?

a. All three techniques begin and end with a cleansing breath.

b. All but the pant-blow technique begin and end with a cleansing breath.

c. They all require the client to breathe in through the nose and out through the mouth.

d. The techniques are not effective during transition.

d
Application
Analysis
Promotion: Growth and
    Development

17-27. A client has been in labor for several hours. She tells the nurse her contractions are getting harder and that she is getting tired. She is becoming very anxious and asks the nurse not to leave her alone. The nurse prepares to perform a vaginal examination and notes some bloody show. Considering the client's behavior, the nurse anticipates that her cervical dilation will be

a. 0 to 2 centimeters.

b. 2 to 3 centimeters.

c. 4 to 7 centimeters.

d. 8 to 10 centimeters.

c
Knowledge
Assessment
Promotion: Prevention and
    Early Detection

17-28. For a low-risk woman during the latent phase of labor, the fetal heart rate should be assessed every

a. 15 minutes.

b. 30 minutes.

c. 1 hour.

d. 2 hours.

d
Comprehension
Planning
Safe Environment:
    Management of Care

17-29. For which of the following should the nurse obtain informed consent? When
a. increasing the rate of a client's IV.
b. changing soiled bed linens.
c. putting on gloves to perform perineal care.
d. inserting a urinary catheter.

d
Comprehension
Planning
Promotion: Growth and
    Development

17-30. The most effective way to teach a woman about the electronic fetal monitor is to
a. give her a pamphlet to read before coming to the labor suite.
b. teach her about fetal monitoring in childbirth preparation classes.
c. give factual information in the admission interview and answer any questions.
d. demonstrate how it works while it is being applied, and explain the tracing.

c
Application
Analysis/Diagnosis
Promotion: Growth and
    Development

17-31. A woman tells the nurse that her contractions are coming about every 3 minutes and lasting about 60 seconds. Further examination by the nurse produces the following data: fetal heart rate 140 beats per minute; cervix 100 percent effaced and 6 cm dilated; presenting part at station 0; membranes intact. Based on these findings, what phase of labor is the woman in?
a. transition
b. active
c. latent
d. second stage

Chapter 18
Maternal Analgesia and Anesthesia

a

Knowledge

Planning

Physiological:
    Pharmacological and
    Parenteral

18-1. The systemic drug classification most likely to be used to control pain during the active phase of labor is

    a. narcotic analgesic.

    b. opiate agonist.

    c. amide anesthetic.

    d. sedative.

c

Comprehension

Planning

Physiological:
    Pharmacological and
    Parenteral

18-2. Analgesics are not usually administered to a primipara prior to the establishment of active labor, primarily because they might

    a. cause fetal depression.

    b. not be effective at the end of active labor.

    c. prolong the labor.

    d. lead to maternal hypotension.

c

Application

Planning

Physiological:
    Pharmacological and
    Parenteral

18-3. A woman has had a spontaneous rupture of membranes and is having mild contractions every 15 minutes lasting for 30 seconds. She and her partner have completed a prepared childbirth course, and they tell the nurse that they want a medication-free birth. When discussing medication alternatives with the couple, the nurses should be sure they understand that

    a. in order to respect their wishes, medication will be offered only if it is needed.

    b. adequate pain relief will help them enjoy the birth experience more.

    c. maternal pain and stress can have a more adverse effect on the fetus than would a small amount of an analgesic.

    d. medication will allow the woman to rest and be less fatigued after the birth, so she will bond well with the baby.

18-4. A woman is unable to cope with her uterine contractions. Her cervix is dilated to 5 cm. When the nurse suggests the use of a systemic analgesic to make her more comfortable, she asks, "Will my baby get the medicine too?" The nurse's best reply would be,

a. "Some of the medication does go to the baby. However, we are giving it well in advance, so it should be out of the baby's system at the time of birth."

b. "Some of the medication does go through the placenta, but your baby will metabolize it rapidly through her liver and kidneys."

c. "This medication does not cross the placenta, so your baby will not be medicated."

d. "We will give you an intramuscular injection. That will cross the placenta more slowly than intravenous medication."

18-5. The nurse assesses a woman and her fetus prior to administering a pharmacologic analgesic. Which of the following findings would be a contraindication to administering the analgesic?

a. The fetal heart rate is 110 bpm; short term variability has decreased over the last 10 minutes.

b. Clear amniotic fluid leaks from the client's vagina during contractions.

c. The client's strong contractions are 10 minutes apart and last 60 seconds.

d. The client's cervix is dilated to 7 cm, is 100 percent effaced, and station of the presenting part is +1.

18-6. How is regional analgesia *different* from regional anesthesia? Regional analgesia

a. may be administered epidurally.

b. provides pain relief.

c. uses a narcotic agent such as Fentanyl.

d. can be used during labor and after birth.

18-7. During labor the nurse frequently assesses the laboring client's vital signs *primarily* because

a. the administration of an anesthetic agent is very likely to induce neurogenic shock.

b. an increase in pulse, respirations, and blood pressure indicates that the client is in pain.

c. changes in vital signs tend to occur during labor.

d. alterations in the functioning of the mother's cardiopulmonary system affect fetal well-being.

c

Application

Analysis

Physiological:
    Pharmacological and
    Parenteral

18-8. A laboring client tells the nurse that she feels like pushing. A vaginal examination reveals that the cervix is completely dilated and the client is about to deliver. It has been 1 hour since the client received a narcotic analgesic. Based on these data, for what potential complication should the nurse prepare?

a. maternal bleeding

b. ineffective pushing

c. neonatal respiratory depression

d. neonatal hypoglycemia

b

Application

Planning

Physiological:
    Pharmacological and
    Parenteral

18-9. A client who is gravida 2, para 1 is admitted in the active phase of labor. She tells the nurse, "I don't remember anything about my last birth. I want to see and enjoy the birth this time. I can deal with the contractions; I just need some relief down below when the baby is coming out." The anesthesia which would best help this client achieve her goal during labor would be

a. systemic.

b. pudendal.

c. spinal.

d. local infiltration.

b

Knowledge

Assessment

Physiological:
    Pharmacological and
    Parenteral

18-10. Administration of the anesthesia via the epidural route provides what type of anesthesia?

a. total

b. regional

c. local

d. general

d

Application

Implementation

Physiological:
    Pharmacological and
    Parenteral

18-11. The nurse is preparing a woman for an epidural anesthetic. Her partner says, "My sister had medicine put in her back when she had a baby, and she had a headache for a week afterwards." The nurse explains that his sister probably had a spinal anesthetic and that one difference between a spinal and an epidural is that the spinal anesthetic

a. can lead to hypertension, which results in a headache.

b. does not penetrate the dura, but contains a medication that causes headache as a side effect.

c. is a longer-lasting medication than an epidural, so the side effects are greater.

d. penetrates the dura and allows a small amount of cerebrospinal fluid to leak out, which can cause headache.

d

Application

Implementation

Physiological:
    Pharmacological and
    Parenteral

18-12. Prior to administration of an epidural anesthetic, what is the best explanation for the nurse to give to the woman and her partner?

a. "Medication will be injected into your spine to relieve the pain."

b. "Medication will be given to numb the area where the pain is coming from."

c. "Don't worry. You won't feel a thing after the medication is injected."

d. "The medication is placed through a tube in your back. It keeps the pain from your uterus from reaching your brain."

a

Comprehension

Planning

Physiological:
    Pharmacological and
    Parenteral

18-13. A woman receives a regional block prior to the birth of her baby. The nurse cautions her that she must lie flat for 6 to 12 hours. Which route was probably used for the woman's anesthetic?

a. spinal

b. epidural

c. pudendal

d. local

c

Application

Evaluation

Physiological:
    Pharmacological and
    Parenteral

18-14. The most common adverse effect of using continuous epidural anesthesia during labor make it essential for the nurse to assess for

a. maternal respiratory depression.

b. maternal hypertension.

c. fetal heart rate changes.

d. precipitous birth of the baby.

a

Comprehension

Planning

Physiological:
    Pharmacological and
    Parenteral

18-15. The physician orders the administration of an inhalation anesthetic to relax the cervix and facilitate forceps delivery of the fetus. Nursing actions should include

a. maintaining the intravenous infusion.

b. removing the woman's hip wedge for supine positioning.

c. inserting an endotracheal tube.

d. inserting an indwelling urinary catheter.

b
Application
Assessment
Physiological:
  Pharmacological and
  Parenteral

18-16. A woman is in second stage labor. As the baby begins to crown, the physician administers local infiltration anesthesia in preparation for making an episiotomy. The nurse should

a. assess the woman's blood pressure more frequently now.

b. continue to assess vital signs and fetal heart rate the same as before the infiltration anesthesia.

c. watch more closely for fetal heart rate decelerations and loss of variability.

d. assess the client's pulse and respirations every 2 minutes for the next 20 minutes.

a
Comprehension
Assessment
Physiological:
  Pharmacological and
  Parenteral

18-17. A woman received epidural anesthesia during her labor. This increases the risk that she will experience _____ during the fourth stage recovery period.

a. bladder distention

b. nausea and vomiting

c. uterine atony

d. thrombophlebitis

a
Comprehension
Evaluation
Physiological:
  Pharmacological and
  Parenteral

18-18. To evaluate a laboring client for the most likely side effects of an epidural anesthetic, the nurse should monitor her

a. blood pressure.

b. respiratory rate.

c. deep tendon reflexes.

d. urine output.

c
Comprehension
Planning
Physiological:
  Pharmacological and
  Parenteral

18-19. When administering butorphanol (Stadol) for relief of labor pain, the nurse should

a. give it with crackers to prevent nausea and vomiting.

b. assess for hyperventilation.

c. raise the side rails and instruct the woman to remain in bed.

d. assess for urinary retention.

c
Application
Evaluation
Physiological:
  Pharmacological and
  Parenteral

18-20. A gravida 2, para 1 client is in active labor. She has just been given an epidural anesthetic. Which of the following behaviors should the nurse expect from this client during second stage labor contractions?

a. crying out

b. falling asleep

c. pushing, with help

d. ambulating, with help

b

Application

Evaluation

Physiological:
    Pharmacological and
    Parenteral

18-21. After administering butorphanol (Stadol) to a woman in active labor, the nurse judges the *effectiveness* of the medication primarily by assessing the

a. woman's vital signs.

b. woman's coping behavior with uterine contractions.

c. fetal heart rate, pattern, and variability.

d. intensity and frequency of uterine contractions.

c

Comprehension

Planning

Physiological:
    Pharmacological and
    Parenteral

18-22. A laboring woman is correctly positioned for lumbar epidural anesthesia when she is

a. on her side, in the center of the bed, with her back curved.

b. lying prone with a pillow under her chest.

c. on her side, at the edge of the bed, with her back straight.

d. in left lateral position, with bottom leg straight and top leg slightly flexed.

b

Application

Implementation

Physiological:
    Pharmacological and
    Parenteral

18-23. After a woman receives intramuscular butorphanol (Stadol), her labor progresses rapidly. Her baby is born less than hour after the injection and has mild respiratory depression. Which medication should the nurse obtain from the emergency drawer?

a. fentanyl (Sublimaze)

b. naloxone (Narcan)

c. butorphanol tartrate (Stadol)

d. pentobarbital (Nembutal)

a

Application

Assessment

Physiological:
    Pharmacological and
    Parenteral

18-24. After administration of an epidural anesthetic to a woman in active labor, it is *most* important that the nurse assess immediately for maternal

a. hypotension.

b. headache.

c. urinary retention.

d. bradycardia.

c

Comprehension

Planning

Physiological:
    Pharmacological and
    Parenteral

18-25. A woman was admitted for a placenta previa. She is to have a cesarean delivery under general anesthesia. Nursing actions to prepare her for anesthesia include positioning her

a. in supine position, with arms restrained.

b. with a wedge under her left hip.

c. with a wedge under her right hip.

d. on her left side (Sims' position).

b

Comprehension

Planning

Physiological:
Pharmacological and
Parenteral

18-26. If administered with 2 to 4 hours before birth, an intramuscular narcotic analgesic may

a. serve the same purpose as preoperative sedation.

b. result in neonatal respiratory distress.

c. enhance the birth process.

d. prevent the need for an episiotomy.

a

Application

Implementation

Physiological:
Pharmacological and
Parenteral

18-27. A woman had an epidural anesthetic during labor and birth. After the birth, the anesthesiologist left the epidural catheter in place and injected Duramorph into the woman's epidural space. Four hours later, she complains of severe itching. The nurse should

a. recognize this as a common side effect and follow the protocol for administering diphenhydramine HCI (Benadryl).

b. call the anesthesiologist to come and re-dose the epidural catheter with morphine sulfate (Duramorph).

c. recognize this as a serious symptom and call the anesthesiologist to remove the epidural catheter.

d. remove the epidural catheter, put a small adhesive bandage on the site, and call the anesthesiologist.

Chapter 19
Childbirth at Risk

c

Comprehension

Assessment

Promotion: Growth and
Development

19-1. Which of the following statements BEST describes the relationship between anxiety and labor?

a. Increased utilization of glucose stores, caused by stress and anxiety, decrease the availability of glucose to the contracting uterus.

b. Peripheral vasoconstriction, caused by norepinephrine, decreases the blood supply to the contracting uterus.

c. Anxiety, fear and labor pain result in catecholamine release, which can ultimately result in myometrial dysfunction and ineffectual labor.

d. Epinephrine inhibits myometrial activity and, therefore, uterine contractility.

d

Knowledge

Assessment

Promotion: Growth and
Development

19-2. A precipitous labor is one that

a. occurs without the mother's awareness.

b. occurs before the expected date of birth.

c. is of 2 hours duration or less.

d. is of 3 hours duration or less.

d

Application

Assessment

Physiological: Physiological
Adaptation

19-3. A woman is admitted to the birth setting in active labor. She reports that she has been having some bright red bleeding since her contractions began. The nurse monitors maternal vital signs at frequent intervals. The primary reason for this action is to assess for the presence of

a. anxiety.

b. hypertension.

c. pain.

d. hemorrhage.

c

Comprehension

Assessment

Physiological: Reduction of
Risk Potential

19-4. For a labor client who is having some bright red vaginal bleeding, the best method of assessing fetal response is by using the

a. fetoscope.

b. Doppler stethoscope.

c. external fetal monitor.

d. internal fetal monitor.

a

Comprehension

Planning

Physiological: Reduction of
    Risk Potential

19-5.   A woman at 35 weeks' gestation has had 2 episodes of painless, slight-to-moderate, bright red vaginal bleeding. Expectant management will be used in her care. The goal of this approach is to

a. delay the birth until 37 weeks gestation.

b. provide additional emotional support.

c. carefully monitor cervical dilatation.

d. prevent infection and dehydration.

a

Application

Implementation

Psychosocial: Coping and
    Adaptation

19-6.   A physician diagnoses a total placenta previa, explains the situation to the client, and leaves to arrange for a cesarean birth. The client's eyes are filled with tears. Which of the following actions should the nurse do FIRST?

a. take the client's hand and reassure her she will stay with her.

b. ask the physician to come back and talk with the client again.

c. ask the client if she has a family member the nurse can contact.

d. begin to gather the equipment needed to prepare for the cesarean birth.

b

Comprehension

Analysis/Diagnosis

Physiological: Reduction of
    Risk Potential

19-7.   A woman is exhibiting some symptoms of disseminating intravascular coagulation (DIC). The physician orders the appropriate blood tests. Which of the following results would be indicative of DIC?

a. increased platelet count

b. low fibrinogen level

c. decreased (lower) prothrombin time

d. low hemoglobin

d

Comprehension

Planning

Physiological: Physiological
    Adaptation

19-8.   A client at 39 weeks' gestation was diagnosed as having a mild placental separation. She is being admitted to the labor and birth area, but is not having uterine contractions. The nurse will plan her care based on her expectation that the client will

a. need an immediate cesarean section.

b. be kept on bed rest and under close observation until she goes into labor.

c. be kept on bed rest and given tocolytics to prevent early labor.

d. have her labor induced by rupture of her membranes and administration of oxytocin.

c

Application

Assessment

Promotion: Growth and
    Development

19-9.   A primigravida is admitted to the birth setting in early labor. Her cervix is 3 cm dilated, head at -2 station, with intact membranes. The fetal heart rate (FHR) is 154 by auscultation with the fetoscope. About an hour after admission the client's membranes rupture spontaneously. After the initial action of auscultating the FHR, the nurse should next

a. assess present cervical dilation.

b. palpate for frequency, intensity, and duration of contractions.

c. auscultate the FHR after each of the next few contractions.

d. document the client's response to the amniotomy.

d

Application

Assessment

Physiological: Physiological
    Adaptation

19-10.   A primigravida is admitted to the birth setting in early labor. She is 3 cm dilated, head at -2 station, with intact membranes. The fetal heart rate (FHR) is 154. After her membranes rupture spontaneously, the FHR drops to 100 beats per minute, with moderate variable decelerations. The *initial* nursing response should be to

a. administer oxygen per nasal cannula.

b. change the client's position in bed.

c. notify the physician.

d. perform a vaginal examination.

d

Application

Planning

Physiological: Physiological
    Adaptation

19-11.   After a woman's membranes rupture spontaneously, the fetal heart rate drops to 100 beats per minute. The nurse performs a vaginal exam and palpates a loop of prolapsed umbilical cord beside the fetal head. The nurse has the woman's partner assist the woman into a knee-chest position while the nurse keeps her examining fingers in the woman's vagina. The rationale for this action is to

a. help the fetal head descend faster.

b. prevent head compression during contractions.

c. facilitate rapid dilation of the cervix.

d. use gravity and manipulation to relieve compression of the cord.

c
Application
Implementation
Psychosocial: Coping and
    Adaptation

19-12. After a prolapse of the fetal umbilical cord, a woman has an emergency cesarean section under general anesthesia, but the infant is stillborn. Which of the following nursing actions would facilitate the grief process for the woman and her partner?

a. Leave the couple alone so they can express their grief in private.

b. Explain that it is impossible to predict when a prolapsed cord will occur, so there was no way to be prepared for the emergency.

c. Encourage the parents to express their feelings, and explain that they may experience different feelings.

d. Tell the couple that you have arranged for them to be moved to a room on a medical surgical unit.

c
Knowledge
Planning
Promotion: Growth and
    Development

19-13. A fetus is in breech presentation and it has been decided to have the woman give birth vaginally. It will be most important during labor that the woman

a. have an epidural anesthetic/analgesic.

b. is adequately hydrated with intravenous fluids.

c. not push before her cervix is completely dilated.

d. remain ambulatory until her membranes rupture.

a
Application
Implementation
Physiological: Physiological
    Adaptation

19-14. A laboring multipara is having intense uterine contractions with hardly any uterine relaxation between contractions. Vaginal examinations reveal rapid cervical dilation and fetal descent. The nurse should

a. notify the physician of these findings.

b. place the woman in knee-chest position.

c. turn off the lights to make it easier for the woman to relax.

d. assemble supplies to prepare for a cesarean birth.

d
Knowledge
Planning
Promotion: Growth and
    Development

19-15. The nurse may help a client rotate a fetus that is in a persistent left occiput posterior position by

a. having the woman assume a dorsal recumbent position.

b. applying counterpressure in the sacral area.

c. helping the client ambulate during early labor.

d. having the client assume a knee-chest position.

c
Comprehension
Assessment
Physiological: Reduction of
  Risk Potential

19-16. Which of the following women should be observed most
closely at birth for lacerations of the cervix or vagina? One
who
a. is a multipara.
b. has had a prolonged labor.
c. is a young nullipara.
d. has a placenta previa.

a
Comprehension
Assessment
Physiological: Reduction of
  Risk Potential

19-17. A woman is in labor. The fetus is in breech presentation.
When the woman's membranes rupture spontaneously, it is
most important that the nurse immediately
a. check for cord prolapse.
b. observe for the presence of meconium.
c. take the woman's vital signs.
d. check fetal heart rate variability.

a
Application
Analysis/Diagnosis
Physiological: Physiological
  Adaptation

19-18. A woman has been in labor for 14 hours. Her cervix is dilated
to 3 cm and 80 percent effaced. The fetal presenting part is not
engaged. The nurse should suspect
a. cephalopelvic disproportion (CPD).
b. breech malpresentation.
c. intrauterine fetal death.
d. abruptio placentae.

b
Application
Implementation
Promotion: Growth and
  Development

19-19. A woman has just given birth. During labor the fetus was in
brow presentation, but after a prolonged labor, converted to
face presentation and delivered vaginally with forceps assist.
The nurse should explain to the parents that
a. the infant will need to be observed for meconium
aspiration.
b. facial edema and head molding will subside in a few days.
c. the infant will have prophylactic antibiotics.
d. breastfeeding will need to be delayed for a day or two.

a
Knowledge
Assessment
Promotion: Growth and
  Development

19-20. The complication, common to both the mother and the fetus,
which can result from a prolonged labor is
a. infection.
b. hemorrhage.
c. cerebral edema.
d. hypovolemia.

a
Application
Analysis/Diagnosis
Physiological: Physiological
    Adaptation

19-21. A primigravida was admitted in early labor. Her membranes were intact and her contractions were occurring every 5 minutes and lasting about 45 seconds. She says they are very painful, and she is unable to relax between contractions. Three hours after admission, her cervical status remains unchanged. Her contractions now are every 5 to 7 minutes and last 30 seconds. The fetal heart rate is 160 beats per minute. Of the preceding data, which cue suggests a hypotonic labor pattern?

a. Cervical status remains unchanged.

b. Client is in the latent first phase of labor.

c. Uterine contractions are painful.

d. Client's membranes are intact.

b
Comprehension
Assessment
Promotion: Prevention and
    Early Detection

19-22. A woman in labor is at 42 weeks' gestation. When the woman's membranes rupture spontaneously, it is MOST important that the nurse

a. check for cord prolapse.

b. observe for the presence of meconium.

c. take the mother's vital signs.

d. check fetal heart rate variability.

c
Knowledge
Assessment
Physiological: Reduction of
    Risk Potential

19-23. Which of the following is a risk factor for developing disseminating intravascular coagulation (DIC)?

a. cesarean birth

b. multiparity

c. pregnancy-induced hypertension

d. diabetes

b
Application
Analysis/Diagnosis
Physiological: Physiological
    Adaptation

19-24. How are placenta previa and abruptio placentae *similar*? Both

a. cause severe, steady pain.

b. cause uterine bleeding, possibly hemorrhage.

c. begin suddenly and dramatically, with no warning.

d. are associated with a firm, hard uterus.

c
Comprehension
Assessment
Physiological: Reduction of
    Risk Potential

19-25. A 33-year-old multigravida was admitted to the birth setting in the active phase of labor. During the admission assessment, she tells the nurse she has been having some bright red bleeding since her contractions began. Which part of the physical assessment should the nurse *omit*?

a. taking the client's vital signs.

b. auscultating for fetal heart tones.

c. performing a vaginal exam to determine cervical dilation.

d. assessing frequency, intensity, and duration of contractions.

b

Application

Planning

Physiological:
  Pharmacological and
  Parenteral

19-26. A woman has been having mild contractions since 5 a.m. At 8 a.m. her cervical dilatation was 5 cm. At 11 a.m. it is still 5 cm. Her contractions are irregular and mild to moderate in intensity. Medical evaluation shows no cephalopelvic disproportion. The nurse should anticipate preparation for

a. the possibility of a fetal death.

b. oxytocin (Pitocin) augmentation of labor.

c. Doppler flow studies and possible amnioinfusion.

d. intravenous infusion of magnesium sulfate.

b

Application

Assessment

Physiological: Reduction of
  Risk Potential

19-27. Only one umbilical artery is found in an infant's umbilical cord. The nurse should now be especially alert for

a. neonatal infection.

b. neonatal anomalies.

c. maternal drug use.

Chapter 20
Birth-Related Procedures

d

Application

Assessment

Promotion: Prevention and
    Early Detection

20-1. Which of the following Bishop scores suggests the best chance of a successful elective induction of labor? A score of
a. 0.
b. 3.
c. 6.
d. 9.

d

Comprehension

Implementation

Physiological:
    Pharmacological and
    Parenteral

20-2. After inserting prostaglandin gel for cervical ripening, the nurse should
a. apply an internal fetal monitor for continuous FHR monitoring.
b. insert an indwelling urinary catheter and monitor hourly urine output.
c. withhold oral fluids and administer intravenous fluids.
d. position the client supine with a wedge under her right hip.

d

Application

Implementation

Physiological:
    Pharmacological and
    Parenteral

20-3. A woman is having amnioinfusion to treat oligohydramnios. An appropriate nursing action would be to
a. tell her that she cannot have anything to eat or drink now.
b. place a wedge under her right hip and ask her to remain supine for about 30 minutes.
c. remind her to turn on her call light if she needs to get up to go to the bathroom.
d. explain to her that she will need to remain in bed now.

a

Comprehension

Planning

Physiological: Reduction of
    Risk Potential

20-4. A woman has just been told that she must have an emergency cesarean birth. She says, "I'm scared of surgery. Isn't it more dangerous for me than a vaginal birth? I'm afraid I will die." In formulating a response, the nurse should be aware that
a. maternal mortality is higher for cesarean than for vaginal birth, but is still relatively low.
b. most maternal deaths during cesarean birth are the result of anesthesia complications.
c. maternal mortality is lower in cesarean than vaginal birth, but infant mortality is higher.
d. in emergency situations, explanations should not be given until after the surgery is done.

d
Comprehension
Planning
Physiological: Reduction of
    Risk Potential

20-5. Cesarean birth would be an appropriate choice for a woman who has a

a. fear of natural childbirth.

b. history of hypertension.

c. low pain threshold.

d. cephalopelvic disproportion.

d
Knowledge
Implementation
Physiological: Reduction of
    Risk Potential

20-6. The alteration of fetal presentation by abdominal or intrauterine manipulation to accomplish a more favorable fetal position is termed

a. amniotomy.

b. Leopold's maneuver.

c. ballottement.

d. version.

a
Application
Evaluation
Physiological: Physiological
    Adaptation

20-7. During an external (cephalic) version, the client begins to scream and thrash about. The most appropriate intervention is to

a. discontinue the version procedure.

b. begin coaching the client in breathing techniques.

c. administer a non-narcotic analgesic.

d. put on some music for distraction.

c
Comprehension
Planning
Promotion: Growth and
    Development

20-8. Advantages of amniotomy as a method of inducing labor include that

a. contractions are stronger than in spontaneous labor.

b. there is less danger of a prolapsed cord.

c. fetal monitoring is facilitated.

d. risk of infection is decreased.

b
Application
Assessment
Physiological: Reduction of
    Risk Potential

20-9. After an amniotomy, which of the following assessments is most important for the nurse to make in order to monitor for potential complications of the procedure?

a. maternal blood pressure every 30 minutes

b. maternal temperature every 2 hours

c. fetal heart rate every hour

d. hourly urine output

d
Comprehension
Assessment
Promotion: Prevention and
Early Detection

20-10. Prior to an elective induction of labor, it is most essential to determine
a. the mother's Rh factor.
b. fetal heart rate.
c. station and presentation.
d. fetal gestational age.

b
Comprehension
Planning
Physiological: Reduction of
Risk Potential

20-11. Indications for the induction of labor include
a. transverse presentation.
b. premature rupture of membranes.
c. overdistention of the uterus.
d. positive herpes virus type 2 culture.

a
Application
Assessment
Promotion: Prevention and
Early Detection

20-12. All of the following are important when considering labor induction. The most important criterion for successful induction of labor is
a. cervical readiness.
b. stable maternal vital signs.
c. satisfactory fetal position and station.
d. willingness of family for induction.

d
Knowledge
Planning
Physiological:
Pharmacological and
Parenteral

20-13. The nurse is preparing a teaching pamphlet on oxytocin (Pitocin) induction. Which of the following statements should be included regarding risks?
a. Oxytocin does not increase the risk of uterine rupture.
b. Cervical and/or perineal laceration frequently occur.
c. Irritability of the bladder is common with this procedure.
d. Oxytocin induction may cause hyperstimulation of the uterus.

c
Knowledge
Assessment
Physiological: Reduction of
Risk Potential

20-14. The type of cesarean incision made in the skin across the lowest and narrowest part of the abdomen is called a _____ incision.
a. vertical
b. suprapubic
c. transverse
d. horizontal

a

Knowledge

Assessment

Physiological: Reduction of
Risk Potential

20-15. The type of uterine incision that is routinely made for
uncomplicated cesarean birth is the
a. transverse.
b. vertical.
c. horizontal.
d. suprapubic.

c

Comprehension

Assessment

Physiological: Reduction of
Risk Potential

20-16. Which of the following is a contraindication for induction of
labor?
a. pregnancy-induced hypertension
b. young maternal age (under 20)
c. central placenta previa
d. vertex presentation

b

Knowledge

Assessment

Promotion: Prevention and
Early Detection

20-17. In the Bishop scoring system for evaluation of prelabor status
for elective inductions, 5 factors are assessed. Four of these
are assessments of the cervix. The other is fetal
a. presentation.
b. station.
c. lie.
d. age.

b

Comprehension

Implementation

Physiological: Reduction of
Risk Potential

20-18. Internal (podalic) version is attempted only in
a. adolescents with a breech presentation.
b. multiple gestation, for birth of the second twin.
c. obstetric intensive care units only.
d. response to fetal distress.

c

Knowledge

Assessment

Promotion: Prevention and
Early Detection

20-19. A client is admitted to the birthing unit in the early morning.
Her obstetrician has suggested an amniotomy as a method of
labor induction. Which assessment must be made just before
the amniotomy is performed?
a. fetal presentation, position, and station
b. estimated fetal birth weight
c. fetal lung maturity
d. sonogram for biparietal diameter

d

Comprehension

Evaluation

Physiological:
    Pharmacological and
    Parenteral

20-20. In which labor situation is it essential for the nurse to discontinue an oxytocin (Pitocin) infusion? When the

a. client complains of increasing discomfort.

b. uterine contractions are more frequent than every 4 minutes.

c. contraction duration exceeds 70 seconds.

d. uterus does not relax between contractions.

b

Application

Implementation

Physiological: Basic Care and
    Comfort

20-21. While having an episiotomy repaired, a woman says that it hurts. The physician has only 2 more sutures left and wishes to proceed. What is the nurse's best initial action to help the client?

a. Use positive thinking and say, "It doesn't hurt too bad, now."

b. Place a hand on the client's shoulder and distract her by talking to her.

c. Insist that the physician stop suturing and administer more local anesthetic.

d. Explain that there are just 2 stitches left and that more anesthetic would cost more money.

a

Knowledge

Planning

Physiological: Physiological
    Adaptation

20-22. The most common indication for the use of a vacuum extractor is

a. prolongation of the second stage of labor.

b. prevention of maternal hemorrhage.

c. prevention of fetal abnormalities.

d. prolongation of the first stage of labor.

b

Knowledge

Assessment

Physiological: Reduction of
    Risk Potential

20-23. The criteria for external (cephalic) version include which of the following? The

a. nonstress test (NST) is not reactive.

b. presenting part must not be engaged.

c. membranes must be ruptured.

d. fetus must weigh at least 4000 gm. (8 lb. 13 oz.)

d

Comprehension

Planning

Physiological:
    Pharmacological and
    Parenteral

20-24. A woman has been admitted for an external (cephalic) version. She has just returned from ultrasound and a fetal heart monitor has been attached. Her obstetrician has ordered intravenous terbutaline for the purpose of

a. providing maternal analgesia.

b. inducing labor.

c. preventing hemorrhage.

d. achieving uterine relaxation.

b
Comprehension
Implementation
Physiological: Physiological
    Adaptation

20-25. Which of the following would be an indication for use of forceps during birth?

a. desire for a more rapid delivery

b. maternal exhaustion

c. inadequate pain relief

d. precipitous birth

c
Application
Planning
Physiological:
    Pharmacological and
    Parenteral

20-26. A gravida 2, para 1 woman is 2 weeks past her estimated birthing date, and she has been admitted for oxytocin (Pitocin) induction of labor. In planning nursing care for this client, the nurse will plan for

a. frequent ambulation.

b. limited visiting privileges for the client's partner.

c. assessing maternal vital signs every 15 minutes.

d. evaluating fetal blood gases every 2 hours.

c
Knowledge
Assessment
Safety: Management of Care

20-27. At the end of 1999, the total percentage of cesarean births is believed to be approximately

a. 1%.

b. 5%.

c. 22%.

d. 12%.

Chapter 21
The Physiological Responses of the Newborn to Birth

d
Application
Planning
Promotion: Growth and
    Development

21-1. A new mother says, "I've fed my baby formula three times since he was born and he threw up every time. What is wrong?" The nurse's best response should include,

a. "His stomach is still immature. Let's switch him to glucose water for the next feeding."

b. "We'll watch him closely. Once in a while that can be a sign of a stomach problem that can be fixed with minor surgery."

c. "His stomach is still immature. Don't worry about it. He'll stop doing that in a few days."

d. "That's normal for new babies. Be sure to burp him well during and after the feeding, and don't overfeed."

c
Application
Analysis/
Diagnosis
Promotion: Growth and
    Development

21-2. A 50-hour-old infant has been passing thin, unformed, greenish-brown stools containing a bit of dark, tar-like substance. What conclusion should the nurse draw? These are

a. meconium stools, expected at this time.

b. meconium stools, expected earlier.

c. transitional stools, expected at this time.

d. transitional stools, expected earlier.

d
Application
Analysis/
Diagnosis
Promotion: Growth and
    Development

21-3. A one-day-old infant is awake and lying quietly. The nurse counts the baby's apical pulse at 100 bpm and recognizes this finding as being

a. abnormally low.

b. abnormally high.

c. on the high end of normal range.

d. on the low end of normal range.

d
Comprehension
Implementation
Physiological:
    Pharmacological and
    Parenteral Therapies

21-4. Intramuscular Vitamin K (AquaMEPHYTON) is administered to a newborn just after birth. The mother asks, "Why are you giving my baby a shot?" The nurse should tell her that it is intended to

a. stimulate growth of intestinal flora.

b. promote absorption of fat-soluble nutrients.

c. speed conjugation of bilirubin.

d. prevent potential bleeding problems.

a

Application

Planning

Promotion: Growth and
  Development

21-5. Six hours after birth, an infant is awake and alert. The infant's respiratory rate is 44 per minute. The infant's respirations are shallow with periods of apnea lasting up to 5 seconds. The infant's heart rate is 160 bpm. The infant's skin is pink except for some cyanosis on the soles of her feet. Based upon this assessment data the nurse should

a. continue routine assessments.

b. double-wrap the baby in a warm blanket.

c. request an order for supplemental oxygen.

d. call the clinician immediately and report the assessment.

d

Comprehension

Assessment

Promotion: Growth and
  Development

21-6. Which two neonatal body systems must undergo the most *rapid* changes to support extrauterine life?

a. gastrointestinal and hepatic

b. urinary and hematologic

c. neurologic and temperature control

d. respiratory and cardiovascular

b

Comprehension

Assessment

Physiological: Reduction of
  Risk Potential

21-7. Prior to birth, some fluid is present in the fetus's lungs. Which of the following situations would interfere with the *primary* mechanism of mechanical removal of fluid from the lungs?

a. administration of oxygen via face mask

b. delivery via cesarean birth

c. failure to cry at birth

d. low serum protein level

d

Comprehension

Planning

Promotion: Growth and
  Development

21-8. At the birth of an infant, the purpose of using a mucus trap and suction is to

a. expand the alveoli.

b. increase available oxygen.

c. decompress the stomach.

d. remove fluid from the oropharynx.

c

Knowledge

Assessment

Promotion: Growth and
  Development

21-9. Air entering an infant's lungs immediately after birth affects cardiopulmonary physiology by

a. decreasing pulmonary blood flow and increasing alveolar PCO_2 levels.

b. increasing alveolar PO_2 and pulmonary vascular resistance.

c. increasing alveolar PO_2 and decreasing pulmonary vascular resistance.

d. increasing pulmonary blood flow and PCO_2 levels.

c

Comprehension

Assessment

Promotion: Growth and
    Development

21-10. Because of the high levels of fetal hemoglobin (Hgb F) present in the neonatal period, it is important for the nurse to know that the newborn

a. exhibits the usual clinical signs of hypoxia readily.

b. has greater oxygen available to the tissues than an adult.

c. will not exhibit cyanosis as readily when O_2 blood levels drop.

d. will exhibit cyanosis at relatively high blood oxygen levels.

d

Knowledge

Assessment

Promotion: Growth and
    Development

21-11. Closure of the newborn's foramen ovale occurs when

a. the umbilical cord is severed.

b. blood flows from the pulmonary artery to the aorta.

c. increased PO_2 causes constriction to occur.

d. left atrial pressure exceeds right atrial pressure.

b

Knowledge

Assessment

Promotion: Growth and
    Development

21-12. A 2-day-old, full-term newborn has had an uneventful neonatal course. In assessing the baby's heart rate the nurse should

a. palpate the carotid artery for 1 minute.

b. auscultate the apical rate for 1 minute.

c. palpate the radial pulse for 30 seconds and multiply by 2.

d. auscultate the apical rate for 15 seconds and multiply by 4.

a

Comprehension

Assessment

Promotion: Growth and
    Development

21-13. If a one-day-old infant's vital signs were taken while she was crying, the nurse would expect to find

a. an elevated heart rate and blood pressure.

b. an elevated heart rate and decreased blood pressure.

c. a decreased heart rate and blood pressure.

d. a decreased heart rate and increased blood pressure.

b

Comprehension

Assessment

Promotion: Growth and
    Development

21-14. During the first few days of life an infant's blood tests should reveal hemoglobin and hematocrit values

a. lower than comparable adult values.

b. higher than comparable adult values.

c. that demonstrate shift of fluid to the intravascular compartment.

d. consistent with high O_2 fetal oxygen saturation.

c

Application

Assessment

Promotion: Growth and
    Development

21-15. An apparently normal 18-hour-old infant has a hematocrit of 64 percent. This is most likely due to

a. fluid volume deficit.

b. perinatal bleeding.

c. delayed cord clamping.

d. calorie deficit from breastfeeding.

c

Comprehension

Planning

Physiological: Basic Care and
    Comfort

21-16. Compared to adults, a newborn's ability to maintain a thermoneutral environment requires

a. higher environmental oxygen levels.

b. greater relative muscle mass.

c. higher environmental temperatures.

d. lower environmental temperatures.

a

Knowledge

Analysis/

Diagnosis

Promotion: Growth and
    Development

21-17. Temperature instability in a newborn is primarily the result of

a. excessive heat loss.

b. impaired thermogenesis.

c. immature central control (hypothalamus).

d. lack of glycogen stores.

a

Comprehension

Assessment

Promotion: Growth and
    Development

21-18. Which of the following physical characteristics serves to decrease a newborn's loss of heat?

a. flexed posture

b. blood vessel dilation

c. limited subcutaneous fat

d. larger body surface relative to that of an adult

a

Application

Assessment

Physiological: Basic Care and
    Comfort

21-19. A newborn's temperature drops when she is placed on the cool, plastic surface of an infant seat. This is an example of heat loss via

a. conduction.

b. convection.

c. evaporation.

d. radiation.

c

Application

Implementation

Physiological: Reduction of
  Risk Potential

21-20. An 18-hour-old, full-term newborn has been being breast-fed since birth. To this point, his neonatal course has been uneventful, but he has not been latching on or sucking well at breast. The nurse performs a heel stick and discovers a blood glucose level of 38 mg/dl. What should the nurse do?

a. recognize this as a normal value.

b. observe for clinical signs of hyperglycemia.

c. institute the nursery policy for the hypoglycemic infant.

d. substitute sterile water feedings instead of formula.

b

Application

Implementation

Promotion: Growth and
  Development

21-21. On the third day after birth, a baby's skin turns a yellow color. Her mother asks the home health nurse if the baby has "that contagious liver disease." The nurse's best response would be

a. "Don't be silly. You know that your baby hasn't received a blood transfusion."

b. "I can tell that you are worried about your baby. Let me talk to you about this temporary change in her appearance."

c. "Just let me worry about her skin color-you concentrate on learning how to bathe and feed her."

d. "She has a condition known as physiologic jaundice. You will need to make an appointment to see the doctor this week."

a

Comprehension

Planning

Promotion: Growth and
  Development

21-22. A newborn's father expresses concern that his baby does not have good control of his hands and arms. It is important for the father to realize that

a. neurological function progresses in a head-to-toe, proximal-to-distal fashion.

b. purposeless, uncoordinated movements of the arms are abnormal.

c. mild hypotonia is expected in the upper extremities.

d. asymmetric muscle tone is not unusual.

b

Comprehension

Planning

Physiological: Reduction of
  Risk Potential

21-23. A woman is admitted to the antepartal unit for observation. She is 30 weeks into her pregnancy, and care is directed at prolonging the gestation period. The nurse knows that if the woman's baby were delivered at 30 weeks' gestation, the greatest threat to the baby's well-being would be

a. inadequate thermal stimuli.

b. lack of adequate surfactant.

c. pronounced thrombocytopenia.

d. reduced capillary permeability.

b
Comprehension
Promotion: Growth and
    Development

21-24. Which of the following is most difficult for a newborn to digest and absorb?

    a. lactose

    b. starches

    c. fats

    d. proteins

a
Application
Analysis/
Diagnosis
Promotion: Growth and
    Development

21-25. The nurse observes that a newborn pauses for 5 to 15 seconds between some breaths. There is no change in skin color. The nurse realizes that

    a. this is normal, periodic breathing.

    b. the infant is experiencing apnea.

    c. this breathing is expected with motor activity.

    d. such breathing is expected during deep sleep.

a
Comprehension
Assessment
Promotion: Growth and
    Development

21-26. The fluid in an infant's lungs *prior* to birth originates

    a. from secretions produced by the fetal lungs.

    b. in secretions aspirated from the birth canal.

    c. from swallowed amniotic fluid.

    d. in capillary fluid which osmosed into the fetal lungs.

b
Application
Assessment
Physiological: Reduction at
    Risk Potential

21-27. A baby was born prematurely at 35 weeks' gestation. Realizing that he may have a surfactant deficiency, the nurse would observe specifically for

    a. generalized jaundice.

    b. grunting and sternal retractions.

    c. abdominal distention.

    d. frothy, blood-tinged sputum.

b
Application
Implementation
Promotion: Growth and
    Development

21-28. A 2-day-old, full-term newborn has had an uneventful neonatal course. Her mother seems anxious. She tells the nurse, "Dr Anders said he heard a heart murmur when he listened to my baby's chest. Is that serious?" Which statement by the nurse reflects accurate knowledge?

    a. "All babies have heart murmurs. Don't worry about her."

    b. "Most heart murmurs in young babies are not serious and disappear in a short time."

    c. "Your baby most likely has a tiny hole in her heart."

    d. "Your baby will be transferred to the neonatal ICU so we can monitor her heart murmur."

d

Comprehension

Analysis/

Diagnosis

Promotion: Growth and
Development Through
the Life Span

21-29. A baby is delivered at 38 weeks' gestation. During the first hour after birth the nurse counts his respiratory rate and finds it to be 40 breaths per minute. This is

a. a little low.

b. a little high.

c. extremely high.

d. in the normal range.

Chapter 22
Nursing Assessment of the Newborn

c

Application

Analysis/Diagnosis

Physiological:
Pharmacological and
Parenteral Therapies

1. The initial newborn assessment includes information about the mother. Of the following information, which would be most likely to have implications for the care of the newborn?

a. maternal age-22 years

b. maternal smoking behavior-nonsmoker

c. maternal analgesia-meperidine (Demerol) 25 mg IV, 15 min prior to birth

d. maternal dietary intake-last meal 4 hours prior to initiation of active labor

c

Comprehension

Assessment

Promotion: Growth and
Development

2. The *most thorough and complete* physical examination of a newborn is usually done

a. in the birthing room immediately after birth.

b. by the nurse, as a second assessment, made 1 to 4 hours after birth.

c. by a physician or advanced practice nurse prior to discharge from the birth setting.

d. in the primary healthcare provider's office at the 4-week follow-up appointment.

c

Application

Implementation

Promotion: Growth and
Development

22-3. A couple is holding their newborn son, who was delivered vaginally less than an hour ago. The father asks, "What is this big lump on his head?" The nurse palpates a localized, soft area, 3 cm by 5 cm in size that crosses the lambdoidal suture at the back of the baby's head. The baby's head appears somewhat elongated, and the swelling is slightly to one side of the posterior fontanelle, adding to that effect. The nurse should reply, "The pressure on the baby's head during labor and birth has caused

a. his head bones to overlap slightly. This is normal."

b. some bleeding between the scalp and the surface of a bone in his head. It will go away within 2 or 3 weeks."

c. some swelling in the baby's scalp. The fluid will reabsorb, and it should go away in a day or so."

d. some bleeding in the baby's scalp. It will go away in a week or so. Meanwhile, don't worry if his skin seems slightly yellow in the next few days."

a

Application

Implementation

Promotion: Growth and
    Development

22-4. The nurse notices that a baby's fontanel swells when he cries
or passes a stool. Later, when taking the baby's apical pulse,
the nurse notices that the baby's fontanelle pulsates slightly
with each heartbeat. The nurse should

    a. recognize this as normal and do nothing.

    b. palpate the baby's head to feel for a cephalhematoma.

    c. notify the physician when the next rounds are made.

    d. notify the physician immediately.

c

Knowledge

Analysis/Diagnosis

Promotion: Prevention and
    Early Detection

22-5. When assessing a newborn's eyes, which of the following is
an *abnormal* finding that should be recorded and/or reported?

    a. "doll's eye"

    b. transient strabismus

    c. blue-colored sclera

    d. small subconjunctival hemorrhages of the sclera

b

Application

Implementation

Physiological: Reduction of
    Risk Potential

22-6. A mother of a 10-day-old infant calls to tell the home health
nurse that since her baby's cord fell off, it has been draining
"some pink, watery stuff." The nurse should tell her to

    a. clean it three times a day with alcohol or hydrogen
peroxide.

    b. call for an appointment to have the primary healthcare
provider treat it.

    c. not bathe the baby in a tub of water until it dries up.

    d. take the baby to the emergency room as soon as possible.

a

Application

Implementation

Promotion: Growth and
    Development

22-7. A newborn is sucking on a pacifier. The nurse notes that the
infant responds to noises by briefly ceasing to suck on the
pacifier and then continuing with the sucking. The nurse
should

    a. document this evidence of normal functioning.

    b. immediately evaluate the Moro and rooting reflexes.

    c. request advanced neurological testing.

    d. carry out additional tests to evaluate for hearing
impairment.

a

Knowledge

Assessment

Promotion: Growth and
    Development

22-8. When should the nurse begin to involve a normal newborn's parents in the newborn nursing assessment process?

a. from the moment of birth, for example at the Apgar scoring

b. when the baby is alone with the parents during the postpartum period

c. when the nurse reports the gestational age assessment to the parents

d. after comprehensive medical-nursing discharge assessment is completed

a

Comprehension

Planning

Psychosocial: Psychosocial
    Adaptation

22-9. For a newborn born in a hospital setting, the *primary* purpose for the nurse to include the parents in the initial newborn assessment process is to

a. promote parental-newborn attachment and begin health education.

b. foster parental independence in providing the baby's care.

c. involve the parents in decision-making regarding his medical care.

d. support positive attitudes toward the baby's ongoing health care.

d

Comprehension

Assessment

Promotion: Prevention and
    Early Detection

22-10. For a baby with an uncomplicated labor and birth, the first gestational age assessment should be completed during the first four hours after an infant's birth because

a. the physical criteria which are evaluated change after that.

b. effects of labor and birth are least notable during this time.

c. separation from the parents is easily accomplished at this time.

d. age-related neonatal problems must be assessed and managed promptly.

c

Application

Analysis/Diagnosis

Promotion: Growth and
    Development

22-11. Which of the following behaviors would the nurse interpret as a *normal* reflex response for a newborn? When the nurse

a. stimulates the baby's palm with her finger, the baby draws her hand away.

b. strokes the baby's left cheek, the baby makes a slight facial grimace and turns her head to the right.

c. strokes the lateral sole of the baby's foot, the baby fans and hyperextends her toes.

d. lifts and suddenly lowers the baby, the baby flexes her arms and legs close to her body.

a

Application

Assessment

Promotion: Growth and
    Development

22-12. Which of the following physical assessment findings would be recorded as part of a newborn's gestational age assessment?

a. plantar creases present on anterior 2/3 of sole

b. umbilical cord moist to touch

c. anterior and posterior fontanels patent

d. milia present on bridge of nose

b

Comprehension

Analysis/Diagnosis

Promotion: Prevention and
    Early Detection

22-13. When estimating a newborn's gestational age, it is important to remember that assessment criteria

a. must correlate with the composite score to be useful.

b. may be affected by some maternal health conditions (e.g., diabetes).

c. are sometimes more accurate in determining gestational age than is the total score.

d. are more useful in assessing postmaturity than prematurity.

d

Application

Analysis/Diagnosis

Promotion: Growth and
    Development

22-14. The nurse notes that a newborn's breast tissue consists of a flat areola with no bud. This finding is consistent with

a. male gender.

b. a birth defect.

c. decreased maternal hormones.

d. preterm gestational age.

a

Comprehension

Analysis/Diagnosis

Promotion: Growth and
    Development

22-15. In a preterm newborn, a finding of greater neuromuscular tone in the lower extremities than in the upper extremities *most* commonly indicates

a. a normal gestational development pattern.

b. evidence of cephalocaudal fetal development.

c. cerebral palsy affecting the motor cortex.

d. abnormal intrauterine positioning prior to birth.

c

Knowledge

Assessment

Promotion: Prevention and
    Early Detection

22-16. The square window sign is elicited by flexing the

a. foot toward the shin.

b. thigh on the abdomen.

c. hand toward the ventral forearm.

d. neck toward the chest.

d
Comprehension
Analysis/Diagnosis
Physiological: Reduction of
    Risk Potential

22-17. Which of the following is consistent with a diagnosis of postmaturity?

a. ankle dorsiflexion to a 45-degree angle

b. a 90-degree square window sign

c. moving the elbow past the midline of the body when the arm is pulled across the chest

d. keeping the head in front of the body when pulled to a sitting position

c
Application
Implementation
Psychosocial: Coping and
    Adaptation

22-18. A full-term infant's birth weight was 3405 grams (7 lbs, 8 oz). The infant's weight has dropped to 3200 grams on day 3 of her life. The infant's parents are very upset and question the care in the nursery. Which of the following statements by the nurse would be most therapeutic?

a. "Don't worry. All newborn babies lose weight. "

b. "I share your concern. Baby's weight loss is a little excessive. However, the baby will begin to gain weight very soon now."

c. "I can see that you are worried about your baby. Babies are expected to lose weight in the first few days. Your baby has lost only a little weight and should begin to gain weight now."

d. "Your baby eats well in the nursery. Maybe you aren't feeding the baby properly. Let me watch you when you feed the baby the next time so we can be sure."

b
Application
Implementation
Promotion: Growth and
    Development

22-19. An infant was born at term, weighing 3405 grams (7 lbs, 8 oz). The parents question how rapidly their baby should grow. Which response is correct?

a. "Your baby's weight should be triple what it was at birth by the age of 6 months."

b. "It varies, but most babies gain about 7 ounces a week during the first 6 months."

c. "Most babies gain a pound a month for the first 6 months."

d. "Most infants gain a pound a week for the first 6 months."

a

Comprehension

Analysis/Diagnosis

Promotion: Growth and
    Development

22-20. A normal newborn, a first-born, was born at term. The parents are very anxious. The mother asks why the baby's hands are clenched and why the baby's knees and elbows are bent. The nurse's response should be based on the knowledge that

a. flexion is the normal position for the newborn.

b. parental anxiety causes the baby's tension and flexed posture.

c. placing the baby in a supine position will decrease his flexed posture.

d. the baby's muscle tone will relax when he is stimulated appropriately.

d

Application

Analysis/Diagnosis

Promotion: Prevention and
    Early Detection

22-21. When performing a physical examination of a newborn, which of the following findings should be reported immediately to the clinician/physician?

a. overriding of the cranial bones

b. patent anterior and posterior fontanels

c. spongy, edematous area of the scalp

d. head circumference 4 cm less than chest circumference

b

Application

Assessment

Promotion: Prevention and
    Early Detection of
    Disease

22-22. During a newborn assessment the nurse uses a fingertip to press the infant's gum line and the end of his nose. The nurse is assessing for

a. state of alertness and motor activity.

b. evidence of increased bilirubin.

c. adequacy of tissue perfusion.

d. the infant's response to painful stimuli.

d

Application

Planning

Promotion: Growth and
    Development

22-23. A woman is somewhat anxious about the health of her 2-day-old baby. She tells the nurse that she is concerned that the infant sheds no tears when crying. The nurse's response should be based on the knowledge that

a. newborn lachrymal ducts must be punctured to initiate tear flow.

b. silver nitrate and antibiotic instillation at birth reduce tear formation for several days.

c. exposure to rubella in utero can result in lachrimal duct stenosis.

d. lachrimal ducts are usually nonfunctional until two months of age.

b
Comprehension
Assessment
Promotion: Prevention and
    Early Detection of
    Disease

22-24. During a physical assessment the nurse palpates the newborn's hard and soft palate with a clean index finger. This is done to detect

a. a shortened frenulum.

b. openings in the palate.

c. *Candida albicans* infection.

d. adequacy of saliva production.

c
Comprehension
Analysis/Diagnosis
Promotion: Prevention and
    Early Detection

22-25. Which of the following data from a newborn assessment would be interpreted as an abnormal finding?

a. cylindrical, protruding abdomen

b. blinking in response to bright light

c. ability to sleep in presence of loud noises

d. top of ear parallel to outer canthus of the eye

a
Comprehension
Analysis/Diagnosis
Promotion: Prevention and
    Early Detection

22-26. If the newborn does not pass meconium during the first 36 hours of life, more information is needed. The nurse should

a. notify the physician or nurse clinician.

b. perform a digital examination of the anus.

c. increase the amount of oral feedings.

d. measure the abdominal girth.

a
Comprehension
Analysis/Diagnosis
Promotion: Growth and
    Development

22-27. A new mother, asks the nurse, "Why are my baby's hands and feet blue?" The nurse's reply is based on the knowledge that this is a common and temporary condition called

a. acrocyanosis.

b. erythema neonatorum.

c. harlequin color.

d. vernix caseosa.

a
Application
Evaluation
Physiological: Reduction of
    Risk Potential

22-28. The nurse locates a small port-wine stain on newborn's neck, points it out, and explains it to the parents. Which of the following remarks by the parents would indicate that they understand and that no further explanation is needed?

a. "Even though it's permanent, at least it's not too visible."

b. "I hope it goes away soon, so he isn't marked for life."

c. "My grandmother told me not to drink during my pregnancy!"

d. "The doctor must have pulled on him too hard."

d
Knowledge
Assessment
Promotion: Prevention and
    Early Detection

22-29. When using the Brazelton neonatal behavioral assessment tool to assess a newborn, the best results are obtained at what age?
a. 1-4 hours
b. 12-24 hours
c. 24-48 hours
d. 3 days

c
Knowledge
Assessment
Promotion: Growth and
    Development

22-30. Milia is characterized by
a. erythematous macules containing a central yellow or white papule.
b. erythematous plaques with sharply demarcated edges found in skin folds.
c. pinpoint, raised, white spots on the face and especially across the nose.
d. tiny, white papules on the chin, nose, and cheeks.

c
Knowledge
Assessment
Promotion: Growth and
    Development

22-31. The newborn's chest circumference should be approximately
a. 1 cm smaller than the head.
b. 1 cm larger than the head.
c. 2 cm smaller than the head.
d. 2 cm larger than the head.

c
Application
Analysis/Diagnosis
Promotion: Growth and
    Development

22-32. When assessing a 4-day-old infant, the visiting nurse notes that his umbilical cord is shriveled and black. The nurse should
a. notify the infant's physician.
b. clean the cord with alcohol more frequently.
c. recognize this as a normal finding.
d. cover the cord with a small gauze dressing and reassess later.

b
Comprehension
Assessment
Promotion: Prevention and
    Early Detection

22-33. On the initial assessment, how does the nurse determine that the newborn's anus is patent and has no fissure?
a. inspection of the anal area
b. digital examination of the anus
c. auscultating the abdomen for bowel sounds
d. inserting a rectal thermometer to a depth of 1/2 inch

Chapter 23
Normal Newborn: Needs and Care

d
Application
Implementation
Physiological:
  Pharmacological and
  Parenteral

1. A newborn has had erythromycin (Ilotycin) ophthalmic ointment instilled in his eyes. His parents say, "Look how red and swollen his eyes are. What is wrong?" The nurse should reply,

a. "Your baby may have acquired an infection as he passed through the birth canal. We'll culture it to be sure."

b. "It's nothing to worry about. Many newborns have swollen eyes as a result of the pressure during birth."

c. "Sometimes the medication tube irritates the eyelids as the antibiotic is being applied. Your doctor will evaluate it."

d. "Your baby may be a little sensitive to the antibiotic applied just after birth. His eyes should be fine in a day or two."

a
Knowledge
Planning
Safety: Safety and Infection
  Control

23-2. You are placing a baby in a radiant warmer. Where should you place the skin sensor?

a. on the baby's abdomen

b. on the baby's foot

c. on the baby's scalp

d. on the baby's back

a
Knowledge
Assessment
Promotion: Prevention and
  Early Detection of
  Disease

23-3. The *initial* temperature reading should be obtained from a newborn using the _____ route.

a. axillary

b. oral

c. rectal

d. skin sensor

c
Application
Evaluation
Physiological: Reduction of
  Risk Potential

23-4. When the home health nurse is examining a 3-day-old male infant, the mother points out a whitish yellow exudate on the baby's glans penis. Realizing that the baby was circumcised 2 days previously, the nurse should

a. take the baby's temperature and notify the physician.

b. cleanse the penis with water and apply petroleum jelly.

c. explain to the mother that this is granulation tissue and that it should not be removed.

d. gently remove the exudate with a cotton ball and tell the mother to call the physician if it reoccurs.

d

Comprehension

Planning

Promotion: Growth and
    Development

23-5. A baby was born by vaginal birth just 15 minutes ago. The nurse decided to defer instillation of erythromycin (Ilotycin) in the baby's eyes for an hour. The primary rationale for this decision is so that

a. a routine eye examination may be completed.

b. chances of iatrogenic infection will be reduced.

c. signs of hypersensitivity will not be overlooked.

d. eye contact and bonding will be facilitated immediately post-birth.

c

Application

Evaluation

Physiological:
    Pharmacological and
    Parenteral Therapies

23-6. An indication that a newborn may require additional injections of vitamin K (AquaMEPHYTON) is

a. failure to gain weight.

b. fissures at lip margins.

c. bleeding from the umbilical cord.

d. passage of frothy yellow stool.

a

Application

Planning

Physiological: Reduction of
    Risk Potential

23-7. Of the following nursing diagnoses relevant to the newborn, which would require the *most immediate* nursing intervention?

a. ineffective airway clearance related to mucus obstruction

b. pain related to frequent heel sticks

c. altered nutrition less than body requirements related to limited formula intake

d. altered urinary elimination related to post-circumcision status

b

Comprehension

Assessment

Promotion: Prevention and
    Early Detection of
    Disease

23-8. A baby has just been born by vaginal birth. The nurse must formally admit the infant to the health care facility and assess the baby's adaptation to extrauterine life

a. before removing the baby from the birthing room to the nursery.

b. within the first 2 hours after birth.

c. within the first 24 hours after birth.

d. before allowing the mother to attempt breastfeeding.

b

Comprehension

Planning

Promotion: Growth and
    Development

23-9. Shortly after birth, a baby was placed unclothed under a radiant warmer with a skin sensor attached to her abdomen. This action was taken in order to

a. promote optimal visualization of the baby.

b. prevent expenditure of energy to maintain homeostasis.

c. promote drying of the umbilical stump.

d. allow maximum accessibility to the baby.

b
Comprehension
Planning
Physiological:
    Pharmacological and
    Parenteral

23-10. Where should the nurse administer a vitamin K injection to a newborn?

a. subcutaneously, in the abdomen

b. intramuscularly, in the lateral aspect of the thigh

c. intramuscularly, in the buttock

d. subcutaneously, in the anterior aspect of the thigh

a
Application
Planning
Promotion: Growth and
    Development

23-11. The mother of a 2-day-old infant becomes upset while playing with her baby because the baby avoids eye contact, turns away, and has little arm and leg movement. The mother states that perhaps the baby doesn't like her. The nurses response should be based on the knowledge that the baby

a. is exhibiting normal signs of fatigue.

b. is not bonding well with his mother.

c. is exhibiting signs of illness.

d. needs increased calories to maintain wakefulness.

c
Application
Evaluation
Promotion: Growth and
    Development

23-12. Which action by a newborn's father demonstrates that he understands the correct technique for nasal/oral suctioning? He

a. puts the bulb in the center of the baby's mouth and slowly releases pressure on the bulb.

b. puts the bulb in the baby's nose, being careful not to occlude the nares, gently squeezes it, and then releases it.

c. squeezes the bulb, then puts it in the infant's nose, being careful not to occlude the nares, and then releases it gently.

d. suctions the infant's nose every time he suctions his mouth.

b
Application
Planning
Physiological: Reduction of
    Risk Potential

23-13. In the first 12 hours after circumcision of a newborn, the potential problem with the highest priority is risk for

a. infection.

b. bleeding.

c. stenosis.

d. urinary retention.

c
Application
Planning
Promotion: Prevention and
    Early Detection of
    Disease

23-14. A new mother asks, "What is it I'm supposed to do to protect my baby from sudden infant death syndrome?" The nurse should teach the mother that since her baby is a healthy term infant, the baby should be positioned

a. on its back at all times.

b. on either its back or side.

c. on its back except after feeding and then on its stomach for 30-60 minutes.

d. on its back with their head elevated 30 degrees.

a

Comprehension

Planning

Promotion: Prevention and
    Early Detection

23-15. The parents of a newborn express concern about their ability to care for the infant's umbilical cord stump at home. The most effective way to instruct both parents in proper cord care would be by having them

a. squeeze warm water gently over the penis and pat it dry after diaper changes as you observe.

b. explain the steps of the procedure to them.

c. watch an instructional filmstrip on newborn hygiene care.

d. read a variety of pamphlets on care of the newborn.

a

Comprehension

Planning

Safety: Safety and Infection
    Control

23-16. When caring for a newborn who has already had his/her first bath, you should wear disposable gloves when

a. administering vitamin K and eye medications.

b. washing the baby's face after he/she vomits a feeding.

c. changing a diaper.

d. washing the baby after a bowel movement.

d

Application

Implementation

Physiological: Basic Care and
    Comfort

23-17. The home health nurse notices that the parents of a 3-day-old infant have, in addition to clothing, wrapped the baby in three blankets. The baby's respiratory rate is higher than normal, and he is very active. Which nursing action would be most appropriate in meeting the total needs of the baby and the family?

a. Undress the baby and wrap the baby in a single blanket.

b. Remove the blankets and explain to the parents that they should not use more than one blanket.

c. Undress the baby and place the baby in a basin of tepid water to lower temperature as quickly as possible.

d. Explain that the baby's behaviors indicate that the baby is too hot; remain with the parents as they remove the blankets.

a

Comprehension

Planning

Safety: Safety and Infection
    Control

23-18. For the trip home from the birthing center, the newborn would be adequately protected if transported in

a. an approved car seat facing the rear of the back seat of the car.

b. the mother's arms while she is seated in the rear of the car.

c. an infant carrier secured to the rear seat with a seat belt.

d. an approved car seat facing forward between two passengers in the rear seat.

a

Application

Evaluation

Promotion: Prevention and
    Early Detection

23-19. The nurse is evaluating the discharge teaching. Which statement by the parents demonstrates understanding of temperature assessment for an infant?

a. "The baby's temperature needs to be taken only when there are signs of illness."

b. "We need to take the baby's axillary temperature every day at home."

c. "We should take the baby's rectal temperature at home only if she is sick enough to go to the doctor."

d. "The baby's temperature needs to be taken only when the baby feels warm to the touch."

a

Knowledge

Implementation

Safety: Safety and Infection
    Control

23-20. Which of the following policies would be most effective in preventing infection in the nursery?

a. All care personnel must do a 3-minute scrub at the beginning of each shift.

b. All caregivers must wear gloves when bathing a baby and changing diapers.

c. Any caregiver with an infection must wear a mask and gown.

d. Cribs should be kept at least 4 feet apart in the nursery.

a

Application

Planning

Promotion: Prevention and
    Early Detection

23-21. A healthy newborn's initial nursing care plan lists the goal "Airway will remain clear." Which of the following nursing interventions might be utilized to meet this goal?

a. suctioning with a DeLee mucus trap

b. initiating continuous gastric decompression

c. vigorous stroking of the abdomen

d. positioning supine with head slightly elevated

Chapter 24
Newborn Nutrition

a

Application

Implementation

Promotion: Growth and
    Development

1. A mother asks, "Is it true that breast milk will prevent my baby from catching colds and other infections?" The nurse should reply, "Current research indicates that

    a. your baby will have increased resistance to illness caused by bacteria and viruses, but she may still contract infections."

    b. you shouldn't have to worry about your baby's exposure to contagious diseases until she stops breast-feeding."

    c. breast milk offers no greater protection to your baby than formula feedings."

    d. breast milk will give your baby protection from all illnesses to which you are immune."

c

Knowledge

Assessment

Promotion: Growth and
    Development

24-2. In most cases, how soon after birth is colostrum replaced by transitional milk?

    a. 8 hours

    b. 12-24 hours

    c. 2-4 days

    d. 1 week

c

Knowledge

Assessment

Promotion: Growth and
    Development

24-3. In comparison to most prepared formulas, mature breast milk provides

    a. a lower concentration of cholesterol.

    b. more calories per ounce.

    c. greater immunologic value.

    d. more nitrogenous wastes.

d

Comprehension

Assessment

Promotion: Growth and
    Development

24-4. When their feeding habits are compared to breast-fed infants, formula-fed newborns

    a. experience shorter periods between feedings.

    b. digest feedings more rapidly.

    c. commonly desire to eat every 1 1/2 to 3 hours.

    d. commonly go 3-4 hours between feedings.

c
Application
Implementation
Promotion: Growth and
 Development

24-5. When bottle-feeding her son, a mother attempts to burp him after every few swallows of formula. He becomes restless and cries, upsetting the mother. Which response by the nurse is most appropriate?

a. "I think you're burping him much too frequently."

b. "Look at how upset your baby has become. Give him to me and I'll feed him for you."

c. "Your burping technique is good, but try burping him only at the middle and end of the feeding."

d. "He's confused. Put him up on your shoulder to burp him."

b
Comprehension
Planning
Promotion: Growth and
 Development

24-6. A client is bottle-feeding her newborn. The nurse should teach her that when her baby regurgitates small amounts of formula, she should

a. take a rectal temperature.

b. recognize this as a normal occurrence.

c. discontinue feedings for 6-8 hours.

d. report this immediately to the pediatrician.

a
Application
Planning
Promotion: Growth and
 Development

24-7. A mother is bottle-feeding her 12-hour-old infant, who tends to fall asleep before taking enough of the feedings. The mother should be taught to

a. use tactile stimulation to arouse sucking.

b. force-feed until the bottle is empty.

c. skip several feedings to increase hunger.

d. increase the size of the nipple opening.

c
Application
Implementation
Promotion: Growth and
 Development

24-8. A client recently gave birth to her second child. While feeding the baby, she experiences strong uterine contractions. She tells the nurse excitedly, "Something must be wrong. I feel like I'm in labor again." Which response by the nurse correctly describes the physiological response the client is experiencing?

a. "Your breasts are secreting a hormone that enters your bloodstream and causes your abdominal muscles to contract."

b. "Prolactin is speeding the blood supply to your uterus and you are feeling the blood vessel engorgement."

c. "The same hormone which is released in response to the baby's sucking, causing milk flow, also causes your uterus to contract."

d. "You probably have a small blood clot in your uterus which is causing it to contract to expel it."

d
Comprehension
Implementation
Promotion: Growth and
    Development

24-9. A woman recently gave birth to her second child. She successfully began breast-feeding the baby in the birthing room. An appropriate nursing intervention would be to suggest that the mother, for now

a. bottle-feed the baby between breast-feeding sessions.

b. routinely use plastic-lined nipple shields.

c. impose time limits for breast-feeding sessions.

d. offer both breasts at each feeding.

a
Application
Evaluation
Promotion: Prevention and
    Early Detection

24-10. The nurse questions a client to evaluate her knowledge of storing techniques for expressed milk. Which statement by the client would indicate a need for additional teaching?

a. "I'll boil the milk just before feeding it to the baby."

b. "After expressing the milk, I'll need to freeze it."

c. "I'll need to make sure that I have plastic bottles for storing the milk that I don't freeze."

d. "The wrong type of bottle will decrease the breast milk's protective function."

b
Application
Evaluation
Physiological:
    Pharmacological and
    Parenteral

24-11. A client is breast-feeding her baby. Which of the following actions by the client would indicate an understanding of the potential effects of maternal medications on her infant? She

a. requests pain medication 30 minutes prior to breast-feeding her baby.

b. reminds her obstetrician that she is breast-feeding when receiving three discharge prescriptions.

c. reminds her husband to bring her time-released hay fever medication from home.

d. refuses decaffeinated coffee, stating, "I need at least four cups of regular coffee to get me moving every morning."

a
Comprehension
Planning
Promotion: Growth and
    Development

24-12. A woman wishes to breastfeed her baby. However, the infant is premature and will not be able to nurse for at least two weeks. The most effective way to stimulate milk production and establish her milk production is for her to

a. pump both breasts simultaneously with a pulsatile electric pump.

b. pump both breasts simultaneously with a hand pump.

c. express her milk manually from both breasts, beginning with the opposite breast at each session.

d. use an electric pump every 3 hours, alternating breasts each time.

d

Application

Implementation

Promotion: Growth and
    Development

24-13.   A 3-week-old baby is being breast-fed, appears healthy, and is gaining weight. Her mother wonders if the baby should receive iron supplementation, like her friend's formula-fed baby. Which response by the nurse reflects current knowledge about the iron needs of a breast-fed infant?

a. "I'll have the doctor calculate the daily dosage of iron your baby should receive."

b. "For as long as your baby is breast-feeding, if you eat a balanced diet and take multivitamins, she won't require an iron supplement."

c. "If you eat a balanced diet, your baby will not require iron supplements until she is three months old."

d. "If you eat well and take your multivitamins, your baby probably won't need iron supplements until she is 4 to 6 months old."

b

Application

Implementation

Promotion: Growth and
    Development

24-14.   Immediately following birth, a mother asks to breast-feed her newborn. Which of the following nursing interventions is appropriate if the newborn appears healthy?

a. Refuse the request and explain why.

b. Assist the mother to attempt breast-feeding.

c. Feed sterile water to evaluate swallowing first.

d. Aspirate stomach contents before the breast-feeding attempt.

d

Comprehension

Evaluation

Promotion: Growth and
    Development

24-15.   Which behavior by the mother of a newborn indicates good bottle-feeding technique?

a. props the bottle on a rolled towel

b. points the nipple at the infant's tongue

c. enlarges the nipple hole to allow for a steady stream of formula to flow

d. keeps the nipple full of formula throughout the feeding

c

Application

Evaluation

Physiological: Basic Care and
    Comfort

24-16.   A client is breast-feeding her baby. She calls the clinic to say her breasts are engorged. She says, "I just wanted to be sure I'm doing the right thing." Which of the following statements by the client would indicate that the nurse needs to reteach the information about relieving breast engorgement? She says, "I am

a. nursing my baby more frequently to relieve the engorgement."

b. wearing a nursing bra, except at night when I sleep."

c. applying cool compresses just prior to feeding my baby."

d. using a warm shower for comfort."

a

Application

Implementation

Physiological: Basic care and
  comfort

24-17. A new mother is breastfeeding her newborn and wonders if he is getting enough milk. The nurse's response is based on the knowledge that the baby is probably getting enough milk if

a. the baby's stools are yellow or are beginning to lighten in color by the fourth or fifth day after birth.

b. they are nursing at least 4 times in 24 hours.

c. there are at least four to six wet diapers every 24 hours after day 5.

d. the infant's abdomen is full and rounded after each feeding.

b

Application

Implementation

Psychosocial: Coping and
  Adaptation

24-18. An infant's mother states, "I feel so guilty that I was unable to breast-feed my baby." The nurse's response showing the most honesty and support for the mother is,

a. "You did your best. Your baby will not suffer much from the formula."

b. "You really will be able to meet your baby's needs with the formula. Tell me more about your feelings about your breast-feeding efforts."

c. "Breast-feeding is much better for your baby. Maybe you just didn't try hard enough or long enough to be successful with it."

d. "It's really not your fault. Some babies are just difficult to breast-feed. They usually end up being picky eaters later in life as well."

d

Application

Implementation

Promotion: Growth and
  development

24-19. A new mother asks the nurse how many months she should continue to breastfeed her newborn. The nurse explains to the mother that the American Academy of Pediatrics (AAP) and American College of Obstetricians and Gynecologists (ACOG) recommend

a. breastfeeding for at least 3 to 4 months of life.

b. breastfeeding until the mother returns to work in 4 to 6 weeks.

c. that infants be given breast milk or whole milk until 1 year of age.

d. breast milk as the optimal food for the first 6 to 12 months of life.

Chapter 25
The Newborn at Risk: Conditions Present at Birth

c
Application
Evaluation
Psychosocial: Coping and
    Adaptation

1. Which of the following provides data to support that a parent is responding in an adaptive manner during the crisis of having an infant in intensive care? The parent says,

   a. "I'd rather not help bathe the baby; you can do it without hurting her."

   b. "I'd never have got hooked on heroin in the first place if it hadn't been for my stupid boyfriend. I won't see him again."

   c. "Is it okay if I try to feed the baby today, or at least hold her for a while?"

   d. "The night nurse doesn't know what she's doing. She is so bossy. And I am definitely changing doctors."

d
Comprehension
Analysis/Diagnosis
Physiological: Reduction of
    Risk Potential

25-2. The newborn infant of a class B (White's scale) diabetic mother is 25 minutes old. In comparison to infants of class D-F diabetic mothers (who have poor uterine blood supply), this baby is at higher risk for developing

   a. hypocalcemia.

   b. polycythemia.

   c. hyperbilirubinemia.

   d. respiratory distress.

b
Comprehension
Planning
Physiological: Reduction of
    Risk Potential

25-3. A newborn infant of a class B (White's scale) diabetic mother is 25 minutes old. The baby's mother states that she finds it difficult to believe that her baby may have problems, because she looks so "pink and chubby." The nurse's response should be based upon knowledge that these signs are physiologic manifestations of

   a. edema and acidosis.

   b. increased body fat and polycythemia.

   c. gluconeogenesis and hyperbilirubinemia.

   d. muscle hypertrophy and hypocalcemia.

d
Comprehension
Planning
Psychosocial: Coping and
    Adaptation

25-4. A high-risk newborn requires immediate transfer to a distant intensive care nursery. The nurse can best facilitate parental attachment by providing the parents with

   a. a daily phone report of the baby's health status.

   b. a visit from a transport team member after the transport.

   c. verbal explanation of the newborn's treatment plan.

   d. photographs of their baby and a card with his footprint.

d
Comprehension
Assessment
Promotion: Prevention and
    Early Detection

25-5. In assessing the newborn for at-risk status, the nurse should know that

a. any infant with a birth weight of less than 2,500 grams is preterm.

b. the large-for-gestational-age infant has little risk of neonatal morbidity.

c. gestational age is the one criterion utilized to establish mortality risk.

d. infants who are preterm and small for gestational age have the highest mortality risk.

b
Comprehension
Assessment
Physiological: Physiological
    Adaptation

25-6. A preterm infant was born at 34 weeks' gestation. The baby is now two days old and weight is average for gestational age (AGA). The nurse is concerned about the baby's ability to maintain a normal body temperature. The nurse is aware that the baby has limited heat production capabilities, because of his

a. extended posture.

b. small muscle mass.

c. proximity of blood vessels to skin surface.

d. limited amount of subcutaneous fat.

b
Knowledge
Planning
Physiological: Basic Care and
    Comfort

25-7. For growth, an uncompromised healthy preterm infant needs at least _____ oral intake of calories per kilogram per day.

a. 50

b. 110

c. 150

d. 200

c
Knowledge
Evaluation
Physiological: Basic Care and
    Comfort

25-8. A preterm infant's nutritional intake would be considered adequate if there is consistent weight gain of

a. 5-10 grams per day.

b. 10-20 grams per day.

c. 20-30 grams per day.

d. 30-40 grams per day.

d
Application
Analysis/Diagnosis
Physiological: Reduction of
    Risk

25-9. A preterm infant was born at 34 weeks' gestation. The baby is two days old and weight is average for gestational age (AGA). He is being carefully monitored prior to initiation of nipple-feeding. Which of the following data groups would indicate that he is *not* ready for nipple-feeding?

a. gaining weight; coordinated suck-swallow reflex

b. alert; axillary temperature of 98 degrees Fahrenheit (36.7 degrees Celsius)

c. apical heart rate 120; skin temperature 36.5 degrees Celsius (97.7 degrees Fahrenheit)

d. nasal flaring; sustained respiratory rate of 68 bpm

d
Comprehension
Planning
Physiological: Basic Care and
    Comfort

25-10. A preterm infant is just beginning to switch from gavage to bottle feeding. During bottle feeding, it is important to

a. use a firm, larger nipple than for a term baby.

b. position the infant supine, with the head of the bed elevated.

c. burp the baby only at the end of the feeding.

d. limit the feeding to no more than 20 minutes.

b
Application
Analysis/Diagnosis
Physiological: Basic Care and
    Comfort

25-11. Which of the following preterm infants is probably ready to progress from gavage to breastfeeding? One with the following data:

a. weak gag reflex, gestational age 32 weeks

b. rooting behavior, weight 2000 grams (4.4 lb.)

c. nonnutritive sucking not present, weight 1500 grams (3.3 lb.)

d. no rooting behavior, gestational age 34 weeks

a
Application
Planning
Physiological: Physiological
    Adaptation

25-12. A preterm infant was born at 34 weeks' gestation. The baby is two days old and her weight is average for gestational age (AGA). The baby experiences a brief apneic spell and becomes cyanotic. When breathing resumes, the nurse observes sternal retractions and nasal flaring. After determining that the infant does not need to be suctioned, the nurse's first intervention should be to

a. give 100 percent O_2 by mask.

b. prepare for intubation.

c. call the physician or nurse practitioner.

d. initiate cardiopulmonary resuscitation.

d
Comprehension
Analysis/Diagnosis
Physiological: Reduction of
Risk Potential

25-13. Similar to the preterm infant, the newborn with postmaturity syndrome is at high risk for cold stress due to

a. extended posture.

b. absence of vernix.

c. parchment-like skin.

d. decreased subcutaneous fat.

d
Knowledge
Analysis
Promotion: Growth and
Development

25-14. In order for a newborn to be classified as small for gestational age, she/he must

a. weigh less than 2500 g (5.5 lb).

b. be born prior to the 34th week of gestation.

c. have suffered growth retardation secondary to placental malfunction.

d. be at below the 10th percentile on a gestational age/birth weight chart.

c
Application
Planning
Physiological: Reduction of
Risk Potential

25-15. Early provision of enteral or parenteral glucose is of primary importance in the small for gestational age (SGA) newborn to

a. promote weight gain.

b. promote glycogen storage.

c. protect central nervous system (CNS) function.

d. accelerate body fat deposition.

a
Knowledge
Assessment
Physiological: Physiological
Adaptation

25-16. The most common and serious problem associated with fetal alcohol syndrome is

a. central nervous system dysfunction.

b. midface malformation.

c. immune deficiency.

d. growth deficiency.

a
Knowledge
Planning
Psychosocial: Psychosocial
Adaptation

25-17. Which of the following is an expected part of the treatment of the narcotic-addicted pregnant woman?

a. replacement of heroin use with methadone

b. complete withdrawal of narcotics

c. postpone any dietary modifications until withdrawal is complete

d. postpone using antibiotic therapy for infections until the third trimester

a
Comprehension
Planning
Physiological: Basic Care and
    Comfort

25-18. In a newborn experiencing neonatal withdrawal from narcotics, nursing interventions to help the infant achieve a more organized behavioral state include

a. swaddling with hands near mouth.

b. positioning on right side.

c. switching from gavage to oral feedings as soon as possible.

d. maintenance of thermoneutral environment.

a
Comprehension
Assessment
Promotion: Prevention and
    Early Detection

25-19. Most states require screening of newborns for phenylketonuria (PKU). The nurse is scheduling a heel stick for a Guthrie PKU test. The heel stick should be done

a. 24 to 72 hours after initiation of breast milk or formula feedings.

b. no later than 12 hours after birth.

c. before the newborn has the first feeding of breast milk or formula.

d. immediately after the initial feeding of glucose and water.

a
Comprehension
Analysis/Diagnosis
Physiological: Physiological
    Adaptation

25-20. A 2-day-old term newborn has a congenital cardiac malformation with resultant cyanosis. The baby's cyanosis is directly related to the

a. right-to-left blood flow dynamics.

b. size of the malformation.

c. location of the malformation.

d. total functional alveolar surface area.

a
Application
Planning
Physiological: Reduction of
    Risk Potential

25-21. The newborn infant of a class B (White's scale) diabetic mother is 25 minutes old and has a serum glucose of 35 mg/dL. The baby is showing no symptoms of hypoglycemia yet. The nurse should anticipate that the first intervention will be to

a. put the baby to breast, or give an oral formula feeding.

b. start an intravenous of 10-15 percent glucose solution.

c. perform a gavage feeding of formula.

d. take the baby's temperature to assess for cold stress.

d
Application
Implementation
Safety: Safety and Infection
    Control

25-22. When teaching home care to parents of an HIV-infected baby, the mother says, "My baby had diarrhea when I was holding him in my bed with me. What should I do with my sheets?" The nurse should tell her to

a. place them in 2 plastic bags, tie them securely and put them in the trash.

b. wash them in hot sudsy water, separate from other household laundry.

c. wash them in hot sudsy water along with other household laundry.

d. wash them separately in hot sudsy water containing household bleach.

c
Application
Planning
Physiological: Physiological
    Adaptation

25-23. Which of the following preterm infants is positioned to promote optimum respiratory function? One who is

a. supine with the head slightly elevated and a small roll under his shoulders.

b. on his side with his neck slightly hyperextended.

c. supine with a small roll under his neck and the foot of the bead elevated slightly.

d. in prone position with his head turned to one side.

b
Comprehension
Assessment
Physiological: Reduction of
    Risk Potential

25-24. Because of a preterm infant's immature neurologic system, the nurse must closely monitor for signs of

a. malabsorption.

b. aspiration.

c. infection.

d. anemia.

d
Application
Planning
Psychosocial: Coping and
    Adaptation

25-25. A preterm infant was born at 34 weeks' gestation. The baby is two days old and weight is average for gestational age (AGA). The nurse should carefully evaluate behavioral sleep-wake states in order to

a. determine whether the baby can progress from parenteral to oral feedings.

b. schedule administration of the baby's medications.

c. determine whether the baby is being overstimulated.

d. help the parents determine optimal times for interacting with the baby.

a
Application
Assessment
Physiological: Reduction of
    Risk Potential

25-26. Physiologic adaptation is a greater stressor for premature infants than for full-term infants because premature infants' body systems are not fully developed. Therefore, compared to a term infant, the nurse would expect to see

a. earlier and more severe jaundice.

b. symptoms of hyperglycemia.

c. more birth trauma.

d. aspiration of meconium.

d
Application
Implementation
Physiological: Basic Care and
    Comfort

25-27. A nurse has gathered the equipment she will use for a gavage feeding of a newborn. She has a No. 5 Fr. feeding tube, a 10 mL syringe, 1/4 inch paper tape, a cup of sterile water, and the formula. Evaluate her preparation. She

a. has everything she needs.

b. does not need the cup of sterile water.

c. needs cloth rather than paper tape.

d. needs a stethoscope, also.

a
Comprehension
Implementation
Safety: Safety and Infection
    Control

25-28. A woman has AIDS. Her week-old baby is showing symptoms of AIDS as well. During a home visit, the nurse discovers that the baby has had a large diarrhea stool containing some blood. When changing the diaper, the mother spilled some stool on the sink and floor in the bathroom. What should the nurse use to clean the spill?

a. a 1:10 solution of household bleach and water

b. undiluted isopropyl alcohol

c. soap and hot water

d. a 1:2 solution of hydrogen peroxide and water

Chapter 26
The Newborn at Risk: Birth-Related Stressors

a

Knowledge

Implementation

Physiological: Physiological
    Adaptation

1. For a newborn with syphilis, which of the following is a correct nursing intervention?

a. Use isolation techniques until the infant has been on antibiotics for 48 hours.

b. Obtain throat, blood, urine, and lesion cultures.

c. Instruct the breastfeeding mother to treat her nipples with nystatin.

d. Assist with x-ray for aspiration pneumonia or hyaline membrane disease.

d

Knowledge

Implementation

Physiological:
    Pharmacological and
    Parenteral Therapies

26-2. Which of the following antibiotics must be given by slow intravenous infusion?

a. Ampicillin

b. Cefotaxime

c. Nafcillin

d. Vancomycin

a

Knowledge

Assessment

Physiological: Reduction of
    Risk Potential

26-3. For a newborn, the preferred site for obtaining blood for PKU or glucose testing is the

a. lateral heel.

b. middle of the heel.

c. great toe.

d. index finger.

b

Knowledge

Implementation

Physiological: Physiological
    Adaptation

26-4. When performing external cardiac massage on a newborn, compressions should be at a rate of

a. 60 beats per minute.

b. 90 beats per minute.

c. 120 beats per minute.

d. 140 beats per minute.

c

Knowledge

Implementation

Physiological:
    Pharmacological and
    Parenteral Therapies

26-5. To combat metabolic acidosis in a severely asphyxiated newborn, once ventilation is established, the nurse would prepare to administer

a. 10 percent dextrose in water.

b. naloxone hydrochloride (Narcan).

c. sodium bicarbonate.

d. a bronchodilator such as theophylline (Theo-Dur).

b

Application

Assessment

Physiological: Reduction of Risk Potential

26-6. A baby has synchronized chest movements, barely visible sternal (lower chest) retractions, no xiphoid retractions, no nasal dilation, and no expiratory grunting. Using the Silverman-Andersen index, and giving a score of 0, 1, or 2 for each of those areas, the baby's respiratory status would be scored as

a. 0.

b. 1.

c. 2.

d. 4.

d

Application

Implementation

Physiological: Physiological Adaptation

26-7. A newborn has had to be resuscitated because of respiratory depression. The baby's breathing is established by bag and mask and 30 seconds of ventilation have been given with 100 percent oxygen. The baby's heart rate is 50 beats per minute. What should be done next?

a. Perform endotracheal intubation for mechanical ventilation.

b. Continue bag-and-mask ventilation until the heart rate is 80 beats per minute.

c. Continue bag-and-mask ventilation until the baby becomes pink and takes a breath on his own.

d. Begin external cardiac massage (chest compressions) at a rate of 90 beats per minute.

b

Application

Implementation

Physiological: Physiological Adaptation

26-8. After obtaining a fetal scalp blood pH of 7.16, a baby boy is born. After initial oro- and nasopharyngeal suctioning, he begins spontaneous respirations. Which action by the nurse now has priority?

a. Insert an umbilical vein catheter.

b. Dry him quickly under a radiant warmer.

c. Apply continued tactile stimulation to his back.

d. Prepare sodium bicarbonate and epinephrine solutions.

a

Comprehension

Assessment

Physiological: Physiological Adaptation

26-9. A preterm infant is born to a class B (gestational) diabetic mother. The baby suffered a period of asphyxia during birth but responded to suctioning and oxygen. The baby was taken to the high-risk nursery. The nurse is concerned that the baby may develop RDS and should therefore be especially alert for development of

a. grunting respirations.

b. decreasing respiratory rate.

c. increasing serum pH.

d. decreasing PCO_2 levels.

c

Comprehension

Implementation

Physiological: Physiological
Adaptation

26-10. A preterm, male infant was born to a class B (gestational) diabetic mother. He suffered a period of asphyxia during birth, responded to suctioning and oxygen delivery, and was taken to the high-risk nursery where his course has declined. He is now classified as experiencing severe RDS. The nurse should notify the cardiopulmonary therapists to set up a/an

a. ventimask.

b. oxyhood.

c. mechanical ventilator.

d. low-flow nasal cannula.

c

Comprehension

Planning

Safety: Safety and Infection
Control

26-11. For a preterm infant with severe RDS, an important nursing order for the nursing diagnosis of Risk for Infection related to invasive procedures is

a. check proper functioning of suction machine every shift.

b. secure and maintain endotracheal tube with tape.

c. use sterile distilled water in the baby's humidifier.

d. check and calibrate all monitors and oxygen devices every 8 hours.

b

Application

Implementation

Physiological: Physiological
Adaptation

26-12. At the beginning of second-stage labor, the nurse observes that there is meconium staining of the amniotic fluid and a slow, irregular fetal heart rate. The nurse should immediately

a. increase the rate of the maternal IV.

b. report these observations to the physician/clinician.

c. stimulate the newborn's scalp.

d. bag with oxygen after the head is born.

d

Knowledge

Analysis/Diagnosis

Physiological: Physiological
Adaptation

26-13. Presence of meconium in the newborn's lungs

a. prevents air leaks.

b. leads to respiratory alkalosis.

c. prevents air from entering the airways.

d. traps inspired air in the alveoli.

a

Application

Analysis/Diagnosis

Physiological: Physiological
Adaptation

26-14. A term infant, weight appropriate for gestational age, aspirated meconium at birth. Which of the following nursing diagnoses would be appropriate?

a. altered nutrition less than body requirements related to respiratory distress and energy requirements

b. ineffective airway clearance related to increased secretions

c. impaired skin integrity related to hyperactive movements and fragile skin

d. hypothermia related to lack of oxygen to thermoregulation center

b
Application
Planning
Physiological: Reduction of
   Risk Potential

26-15. A small for gestational age (SGA) newborn has experienced cold stress. Which of the following nursing actions should be included in the baby's care plan?

a. Use radiant warmer, institute measures for rapid temperature elevation.

b. Initiate monitoring of blood glucose levels.

c. Monitor rectal temperature hourly.

d. Rapidly infuse 50 percent dextrose IV per standing protocol (or obtain order for).

d
Application
Implementation
Physiological: Physiological
   Adaptation

26-16. A newborn experienced symptomatic hypoglycemia and required an intravenous infusion of dextrose. The infant's blood glucose has stabilized and the physician has changed the infant to oral feedings. As the baby begins oral feedings, the nurse should anticipate that medical orders will include

a. discontinuing of IV after first formula feeding.

b. administering long-acting epinephrine.

c. giving a bolus infusion of 25 percent dextrose.

d. re-instituting frequent glucose monitoring during transition.

b
Application
Implementation
Physiological: Physiological
   Adaptation

26-17. A newborn experienced symptomatic hypoglycemia and required an intravenous infusion of dextrose. The baby's blood glucose has stabilized, and the baby has progressed to oral feedings. In addition to assessing for manifestation of recurrent hypoglycemia, the nurse must intervene to conserve the baby's energy stores by

a. discontinuing heelsticks.

b. decreasing crying episodes.

c. lowering the environmental temperature.

d. preventing nonnutritive sucking efforts.

b
Knowledge
Analysis/Diagnosis
Physiological: Physiological
   Adaptation

26-18. The major concern for the newborn with a high concentration of unconjugated bilirubin is damage to the

a. heart.

b. brain.

c. liver.

d. kidneys.

b
Knowledge
Planning
Physiological: Physiological
    Adaptation

26-19. The parents of a newborn receiving phototherapy request information on how the treatment works. The nurse's best response is based on the knowledge that phototherapy

a. reverses the causative factors of hyperbilirubinemia.

b. facilitates excretion of unconjugated bilirubin.

c. blocks movement of bilirubin from tissues to the blood.

d. reduces the rate of red blood cell hemolysis.

d
Application
Planning
Physiological: Reduction of
    Risk Potential

26-20. A newborn undergoing phototherapy experiences increased urine output and loose stools. The nurse should

a. institute enteric isolation.

b. decrease the amount of time the baby is in phototherapy.

c. recognize this as a normal occurrence needing no intervention.

d. provide extra fluids to prevent dehydration.

c
Knowledge
Assessment
Physiological: Physiological
    Adaptation

26-21. The laboratory evaluation for diagnosis of sepsis neonatorum always includes cultures of

a. rectal secretions.

b. gastric secretions.

c. spinal fluid.

d. nasopharyngeal secretions.

c
Application
Analysis/Diagnosis
Physiological: Physiological
    Adaptation

26-22. A baby is born at 32 weeks' gestation, weighing 4 pounds. Twelve hours after birth, the baby is suddenly lethargic and hypotonic. The baby is pale and dusky, and the baby's skin is cool and clammy. The baby's skin temperature is 96.8°; Fahrenheit; heart rate is 162. The baby is not feeding well and has one diarrhea stool. The nurse should suspect

a. respiratory distress syndrome.

b. meconium aspiration.

c. developing sepsis.

d. hypoglycemia.

a
Knowledge
Assessment
Physiological: Physiological
    Adaptation

26-23. In newborns an early sign of sepsis is

a. hypothermia.

b. hyperglycemia.

c. jitteriness.

d. tachycardia.

d
Comprehension
Implementation
Physiological: Reduction of
  Risk Potential

26-24. Which of the following is an appropriate nursing intervention when using pulse oximetry?

a. Recalibrate the machine every 8 hours.

b. Change the electrode site every 4 hours.

c. Inspect the skin site for burns every 4 hours.

d. Check the disposable sensor at least every 8 hours.

b
Application
Implementation
Physiological: Physiological
  Adaptation

26-25. After intrauterine asphyxia, a baby boy is born. Which of the following is the appropriate initial newborn resuscitation step?

a. inserting a nasogastric tube

b. suctioning the oro- and nasopharynx

c. inflating the lungs with positive pressure

d. positioning the head in the "sniffling" position

a
Application
Implementation
Physiological: Physiological
  Adaptation

26-26. A neonate requires positive pressure mechanical ventilation with high inspiratory pressure. There is a sudden change in the neonate's condition evidenced by cyanosis, decreased breath sounds, and asymmetric chest expansion. The nurse's first intervention should be to

a. summon immediate medical assistance.

b. turn the neonate to the nonventilated side.

c. decrease the pressure setting of the ventilator.

d. remove the neonate from the ventilator and manually ventilate with the resuscitation bag.

d
Knowledge
Analysis/Diagnosis
Physiological: Reduction of
  Risk Potential

26-27. Physiologic jaundice in the newborn is caused by

a. fetal-maternal blood incompatibility.

b. destruction of RBCs as a result of an antibody reaction.

c. inability of the immature kidneys to hydrolyze and excrete bilirubin.

d. inability of the liver to adequately bind bilirubin for excretion.

b
Knowledge
Assessment
Promotion: Prevention and
  Early Detection of
  Disease

26-28. A nurse is preparing to perform a heel stick for a capillary hematocrit. How can the nurse decrease the chance of obtaining a falsely high value?

a. Do not perform the heel stick during or soon after a crying episode.

b. Warm the heel before obtaining the blood.

c. Be careful not to shake the capillary tube after filling it.

d. Obtain the blood within 30 minutes after a feeding.

Chapter 27
Postpartal Adaptation and Nursing Assessment

d

Knowledge

Assessment

Promotion: Growth and
    Development

1. How long does it usually take for maternal role attainment to occur following birth?

   a. 24-48 hours

   b. 1-6 weeks

   c. 1-2 months

   d. 3-10 months

a

Application

Analysis/Diagnosis

Promotion: Growth and
    Development

27-2. A woman had a normal, low-risk, vaginal birth 18 hours ago. Since the birth she has been perspiring profusely and her urine output has been 1700 mL. Her pulse is 70 and blood pressure 138/82. How should the nurse interpret these findings?

   a. This is normal postpartum fluid elimination.

   b. This may indicate an infection.

   c. The client may be becoming dehydrated.

   d. There may be an internal laceration of the cervix.

d

Application

Analysis/Diagnosis

Promotion: Prevention and
    Early Detection

27-3. A woman gave birth 24 hours ago after a long, hard labor. Her urine shows a slight (1+) proteinuria. The nurse's interpretation should be that

   a. she is probably developing preeclampsia.

   b. her kidneys may have been damaged by the long labor.

   c. this is a normal finding that needs no action.

   d. this is probably normal, but could indicate cystitis or pyelitis.

a

Application

Planning

Promotion: Growth and
    Development

27-4. A woman is 36 hours post-birth. Her pulse is 54 when the nurse takes her noon vital signs. The nurse checks her chart and sees that her pulse was 88 during labor, and had ranged from 80 to 100 at her prenatal visits to the clinician. What should the nurse do?

   a. Nothing; this is a normal finding.

   b. Take an apical pulse.

   c. Make a note to inform the clinician when she makes rounds.

   d. Check the client's fundal location and firmness.

c

Application

Implementation

Promotion: Growth and
  Development

27-5. Twelve hours after giving birth, a woman calls you to her room. She is drenched with perspiration and her sheets and pillowcase are wet. Her I & O record indicates that she has eliminated 1,500 mL of urine since delivery as well. What should the nurse say to her?

a. This is uncomfortable, but there is no problem. We just need to be sure that you drink large amounts of fluids so you don't get dehydrated.

b. Its normal for new mothers to do this; but you seem to be putting out more fluids than most women do. Call me if this happens again.

c. Don't worry. This is normal. Your body is getting rid of all the fluid it built up during your pregnancy.

d. There is no problem now, but if it continues, we may want to put in a catheter to keep track of the amount of fluids you are eliminating.

a

Knowledge

Assessment

Promotion: Growth and
  Development

27-6. The process that a mother uses to learn mothering behavior and to become comfortable with her identity as a mother is known as

a. maternal role attainment.

b. maternal attachment.

c. engrossment.

d. reciprocity.

a

Comprehension

Planning

Psychosocial: Coping and
  Adaptation

27-7. In several cultures, practices related to childbirth are concerned with restoring the balance between hot and cold. Realizing this, when a woman from the Hmong culture gives birth, the best nursing intervention would be to

a. support family members in their wish to bring in appropriate food and drink for the mother.

b. offer the mother hot tea as soon as her vital signs are stable.

c. encourage the woman's partner to feed her ice chips during the recovery period.

d. turn off the air conditioning, and open the windows if possible, during the birth and during the recovery period.

b
Application
Implementation
Psychosocial: Coping and
   Adaptation

27-8. On the fourth day after birth of their baby, a new father tells the home health nurse that his partner has not been sleeping well and cries easily, but she cannot say what is bothering her. The nurse should tell him,

a. "You need to bring your wife to the office today for further evaluation. We'll work you in."

b. "Many new mothers are a little weepy and depressed for the first few days after birth. However, if she is still feeling the same after a week or two, she may need to see her physician."

c. "I'll ask your physician to prescribe a tranquilizer. What pharmacy do you want us to phone it to?"

d. "Your physician gave her a prescription for some pain pills at dismissal. Be sure she takes one of these every 4 hours as instructed on the bottle."

d
Comprehension
Assessment
Promotion: Growth and
   Development

27-9. A gravida 1, para 1 woman gave birth vaginally to a 7-pound baby girl at 4:00 p.m. It is now 4:30 p.m. When assessing the level of the client's uterus, the nurse would expect the fundus to be located

a. at the umbilicus.

b. at the symphysis pubis.

c. midway between the umbilicus and the xiphoid process.

d. midway between the umbilicus and the symphysis pubis.

a
Knowledge
Assessment
Promotion: Growth and
   Development

27-10. A woman's postpartum vaginal discharge is dark red and contains shreds of the decidua and epithelial cells. The nurse should describe the discharge in the nurse's notes as

a. rubra.

b. serosa.

c. alba.

d. erythra.

a
Comprehension
Implementation
Promotion: Growth and
   Development

27-11. Five hours after giving birth, a woman is assisted out of bed for the first time. She becomes frightened when she passes a blood clot and notices an increase in her lochia. The nurse should explain to the client that

a. the lochia pools in the vagina when lying in bed; gravity caused increased discharge she ambulated.

b. placental fragments have probably been retained in her uterus.

c. she probably has a uterine or urinary tract infection.

d. the amount of lochia will increase during the postpartum period.

b

Knowledge

Implementation

Promotion: Growth and
    Development

27-12. A postpartum client is bottle-feeding her baby. She asks the nurse when she will start to menstruate again. The nurse should tell her that her menstrual period will begin

a. 4 weeks after birth.

b. 6 to 24 weeks after birth.

c. when ovulation resumes.

d. when the placental site has healed.

c

Application

Implementation

Promotion: Growth and
    Development

27-13. The day after giving birth, a client asks the nurse when the red stretch marks on her abdomen and breasts will disappear. The correct response should be, "The stretch marks

a. will disappear in about 6 weeks."

b. are a result of pregnancy and will not disappear."

c. will eventually fade to silver or white."

d. will disappear with the use of vitamin E oil."

b

Knowledge

Analysis/Diagnosis

Physiological: Reduction of
    Risk Potential

27-14. Two weeks after giving birth, a woman returns to the outpatient clinic to be checked by the midwife. The midwife determines that her uterus is located 2 cm above the symphysis pubis. This is most likely an indication of

a. involution.

b. subinvolution.

c. a response to lactation.

d. a full bladder.

b

Knowledge

Assessment

Promotion: Growth and
    Development

27-15. How soon after birth do vaginal rugae typically return?

a. 1 week

b. 3 weeks

c. 4 weeks

d. 6 weeks

c

Application

Planning

Physiological: Growth and
    Development

27-16. A para 1, gravida 1 client gave birth vaginally to a full-term baby girl a few minutes ago. She seems apprehensive and uncertain what to expect during the postpartum convalescence. Immediately after delivery she begins to shake uncontrollably. The nurse should do which of the following?

a. Notify the physician or midwife.

b. Take her temperature again in 30 minutes.

c. Cover her with a warm blanket.

d. Encourage her to take slow, deep breaths.

a

Application

Planning

Physiological: Basic Care and Comfort

27-17. On the first day after a vaginal birth a client states that she is afraid to have a bowel movement because of the soreness in her perineum. To facilitate a more comfortable bowel movement, the nurse should encourage her to

a. ambulate frequently, eat fresh fruits and vegetables, and drink 6 to 8 glasses of water per day.

b. ask her physician to prescribe a laxative to stimulate defecation.

c. drink 2 glasses of warm water after every meal, then try to defecate.

d. do Kegel exercises twice a day, eat a low-fiber diet, and drink 10 glasses of water per day.

b

Application

Analysis/Diagnosis

Psychosocial: Coping and Adaptation

27-18. During the first postpartal day after a vaginal birth, the nurse notices that a client is talkative but seems to be hesitant about making decisions. The nurse knows that according to Rubin, the client is probably

a. having trouble bonding with her baby.

b. in the taking-in phase.

c. in the taking-hold phase.

d. experiencing postpartum depression.

a

Comprehension

Assessment

Psychosocial: Coping and Adaptation

27-19. Eighteen hours after a vaginal birth, the nurse notices that a new mother is talkative but seems to be hesitant about making decisions. Psychologically, at this time she is probably *most* concerned about

a. eating and sleeping.

b. caring for her new baby.

c. relationships with the grandparents.

d. changes in her lifestyle.

a

Application

Implementation

Physiological: Physiological Adaptation

27-20. A woman delivered her third baby vaginally yesterday. She is breast-feeding the baby without difficulty. When the nurse enters the room to perform a postpartum assessment, the client complains that she is having severe afterbirth pains. The nurse should

a. medicate the client for the pain and delay the assessment.

b. perform the assessment to determine the cause of the alleged pain.

c. have the client ambulate to contract the uterus.

d. massage the uterus to expel any retained blood clots.

c
Application
Analysis/Diagnosis
Physiological: Physiological
    Adaptation

27-21. A para 1 gravida 1 woman gave birth vaginally to a baby about 24 hours ago. Which of the following assessment findings should her nurse consider *abnormal*?

a. fundus firm, 2 finger-breadths below the umbilicus

b. pooling of lochia in the uterus while the client is lying in bed

c. perineum red and edematous; large, painful, red hemorrhoids

d. client complaint of pain when the nurse palpates her uterus

a
Application
Implementation
Physiological: Reduction of
    Risk Potential

27-22. When assessing a client 12 hours after a cesarean birth, the nurse finds no lochia on the client's vaginal pad. The client states that the pad was changed 3 hours ago. What should the nurse do?

a. Nothing. This is a normal finding.

b. Take the client's blood pressure now, and again in 15 minutes.

c. Check the vaginal pad again in 15 minutes.

d. Notify the obstetrician of these findings.

b
Comprehension
Analysis/Diagnosis
Promotion: Prevention and
    Early Detection

27-23. In the period immediately after vaginal delivery, a full bladder is significant because it increases the risk of

a. episiotomy infection.

b. postpartum hemorrhage.

c. episiotomy pain.

d. fluid volume deficit.

b
Application
Planning
Promotion: Growth and
    Development

27-24. A postpartum client complains that she has severe abdominal cramps whenever she nurses her baby. The nurse should explain that

a. the sympathetic nervous system is stimulated when the baby nurses.

b. oxytocin, which causes the uterus to contract, is released when the baby sucks.

c. the cramps will decrease if she massages her uterus before nursing the baby.

d. the cramps will stop when all of the blood clots have been expelled from the uterus.

c

Application

Assessment

Promotion: Growth and
   Development

27-25. A client gave birth vaginally to a 7-pound, term, baby boy 3 days ago. During a routine assessment, the home health nurse notices that the client's vaginal discharge is pink and watery and measures approximately 4 inches on the perineal pad. The client states she has worn the pad for about 2 hours. As the nurse documents the assessment data, which of the following would be the best description of this finding?

a. lochia moderate/alba

b. lochia small/rubra

c. lochia moderate/serosa

d. lochia scant/rubra

b

Application

Planning

Physiological: Reduction of
   Risk Potential

27-26. A client gave birth vaginally to a 7-pound, term, baby boy earlier today. She tells the nurse that she passed a small blood clot when she voided. After checking the client's fundus for firmness, the best response by the nurse would be to tell her to

a. inform her physician the next time he visits.

b. save all future clots expelled.

c. expect numerous clots to be expelled in the next 24 hours.

d. massage her fundus after expelling a clot.

d

Application

Implementation

Promotion: Growth and
   Development

27-27. On the first postpartum day, a new mother states, "It seems odd that I don't feel close to the baby yet. I don't even really feel like he has been born yet." The nurse should tell her that

a. she would be glad to have the social worker come and see her and her husband.

b. research has shown that when the father is present at the birth, maternal feelings may be delayed.

c. maternal feelings are usually not present at the birth of the first baby.

d. these feelings are normal and will change with time.

b

Application

Analysis/Diagnosis

Promotion: Growth and
   Development

27-28. Which of the following behaviors would indicate that a new mother was bonding with her newborn son? The woman

a. asks her husband to give the baby a bottle of water.

b. talks to the baby and picks him up when he cries.

c. feeds the baby every 3 hours.

d. asks the nurse to recommend a good child care book.

a
Comprehension
Assessment
Promotion: Growth and
    Development

27-29. It is important for the nurse to assess how the mother felt about the baby before the baby was born because

a. the feelings the mother had during pregnancy will affect her relationship with the baby.

b. often the mother will be able to sense if the baby has an abnormality.

c. the feelings indicate whether the baby's and mother's schedules are compatible.

d. the nurse will be able to determine if reality matches the mother's expectations.

c
Knowledge
Assessment
Promotion: Prevention and
    Early Detection

27-30. Homan's sign is a test to help detect

a. mastitis.

b. endometritis.

c. thrombophlebitis.

d. cystitis.

d
Comprehension
Analysis/Diagnosis
Physiological: Reduction of
    Risk Potential

27-31. During the first few postpartum days, which of the following temperature patterns would cause the nurse to suspect an infection? A temperature of

a. 99.2° Fahrenheit (37.3° Celsius) that persists for any 2 days during the postpartal period.

b. 101° Fahrenheit (38.3° Celsius) during the first 24 hours after birth.

c. 100° Fahrenheit (37.8° Celsius) that occurs on the second postpartal day.

d. 100.4° Fahrenheit (38.0° Celsius) or above after the first 24 hours postpartum.

a
Application
Analysis/Diagnosis
Promotion: Growth and
    Development

27-32. When a new mother first held her baby, she touched the baby's arms and legs with her fingertips. The nurse should recognize this as

a. normal mother-infant interaction.

b. maternal fear and uncertainty.

c. maternal embarrassment and discomfort.

d. probable difficulty with bonding.

b

Application

Implementation

Physiological: Physiological
    Adaptation

27-33. A gravida 1 para 1 woman gave birth vaginally to a 7-pound baby girl at 4:00 p.m. It is now 4:30 p.m. During the assessment, the nurse finds that although the woman's uterus is firm, there is a continuous flow of vaginal blood. She cannot express any clots. These are the same findings the nurse obtained at 4:15. Given these findings, the nurse should

a. reassure the client that this is normal, and help her change her vaginal pad.

b. notify the client's physician or midwife.

c. apply an ice pack to the client's perineum.

d. massage the client's uterus every 15 minutes until the bleeding stops.

d

Knowledge

Implementation

Promotion: Growth and
    Development

27-34. A woman gave birth vaginally to an 8-pound baby boy. On her first postpartum day, she asks the nurse how long her vaginal discharge will last. The nurse should reply "The discharge will change colors, and will last

a. 2 to 3 days."

b. about 6 weeks."

c. until the uterine lining has sloughed off, in about 10 days."

d. until the placental site has healed, usually 3 or 4 weeks."

b

Application

Analysis/Diagnosis

Promotion: Growth and
    Development

27-35. A woman recently gave birth to her second daughter. She is breastfeeding her new infant without difficulty. On the second day postpartum, the nurse assesses the client's uterus and finds it located 3 cm below the umbilicus. The nurse would expect this finding to be a result of

a. bed rest.

b. breastfeeding.

c. retained placental fragments.

d. overdistention of the uterus.

b

Application

Analysis/Diagnosis

Promotion: Growth and
    Development

27-36. A new mother asks, "Am I holding the baby right?" She watches her own mother burp the baby and then holds the baby in her lap and burps him in the same way. She wonders if her partner thinks she is responding in a motherly way. Which of Mercer's (1995) maternal role attainment stages does this represent?

a. anticipatory

b. formal

c. informal

d. personal

d
Application
Analysis/Diagnosis
Physiological: Reduction of
  Risk Potential

27-37. A woman's vital signs were within normal ranges prior to and during labor. Immediately after the birth, her vital signs are: temperature 99° F, pulse 80, respirations 16, and blood pressure 148/90. Which one of the client's vital signs should the nurse be concerned about?

a. pulse 80 bpm

b. respirations 16 bpm

c. temperature 99° Fahrenheit (37.2°Celsius)

d. blood pressure 148/90 mm Hg

a
Application
Analysis/Diagnosis
Physiological: Reduction of
  Risk Potential

27-38. A woman gave birth to her third baby vaginally yesterday. She is breastfeeding the baby without difficulty. The nurse palpates the client's uterus and finds that it is 2 cm above the umbilicus and located on the right side of the abdomen. The nurse should suspect

a. a full bladder.

b. subinvolution.

c. normal involution.

d. retained placental fragments.

b
Application
Implementation
Promotion: Prevention and
  Early Detection

27-39. A woman gave birth to her third baby vaginally five days ago. She is breastfeeding the baby without difficulty. When assessing the client's breasts, the home health nurse notices a generalized swelling in the upper outer quadrant of the right breast. The client asks what could be causing the swelling. The nurses best response would be, "The swelling is most likely caused by

a. a localized site of infection."

b. a blockage of one of your milk ducts."

c. a harmless fatty tumor."

d. an enlarged lymph node."

Chapter 28
The Postpartal Family: Needs and Care

c

Application

Implementation

Physiological: Pharmacological and Parenteral

1. A woman is unsure whether she wants to have patient-controlled analgesia (PCA) for post-cesarean pain relief. She says she is afraid she will overmedicate herself and be too groggy to care for her baby. The best response to address her concern would be,

a. "If you're too sleepy during the first 24 hours, we will take good care of your baby for you."

b. "You'll like the PCA pump. It allows you to avoid the discomfort of having injections every 3 or 4 hours."

c. "The pump has a time lockout, so you can't deliver another dose until the specified time, even if you do push the button."

d. "The PCA pump will give you more control and make you less dependent on the nursing staff."

c

Knowledge

Planning

Safety: Safety and Infection Control

28-2. After delivery, the nurse is preparing an ice pack to place on a client's episiotomy. The nurse should

a. wear sterile gloves to apply the ice pack.

b. tell her to leave it in place for an hour.

c. work from front to back when placing the ice pack.

d. place the ice pack against her perineum and cover it with an absorbent towel.

c

Knowledge

Planning

Physiological: Basic Care

28-3. After delivery, the nurse places an ice pack on a client's perineum. The nurse should teach the client to remove it

a. when the ice melts.

b. when the pain is relieved.

c. after 20 minutes.

d. after an hour.

b

Comprehension

Planning

Safety: Safety and Infection Control

28-4. A client wants to take a sitz bath at home to relieve her perineal pain. The nurse's teaching should include instructions

a. that she take a tub bath instead of a shower; fill the tub full and bathe and sitz at the same time.

b. that bath water should be emptied and the tub cleaned before the sitz to prevent infection.

c. to draw at least 12 inches of water in the bathtub for the sitz.

d. to fill the bathtub with 4-6 inches of water, sitz, then add water to fill the tub and finish her bath.

d
Comprehension
Planning
Promotion: Growth and
   Development

28-5. To suppress lactation and prevent breast engorgement, one thing the nurse should advise the postpartal client to do soon after birth is to

a. avoid wearing a bra for 7 to 10 days after the birth.

b. begin running warm water over her breasts when she is in the shower.

c. massage her breasts to relieve the aching.

d. place ice packs over her breasts for 20 minutes four times daily.

c
Knowledge
Planning
Physiological:
   Pharmacological and
   Parenteral

28-6. A woman delivered her third baby vaginally 18 hours ago. She has strong afterpains each time she breastfeeds the baby. To promote comfort the nurse should

a. massage the client's fundus before the baby nurses.

b. have the client use a nipple shield when the baby nurses.

c. administer an analgesic one hour before the baby will nurse.

d. have the client perform Kegel exercises while she nurses the baby.

a
Knowledge
Planning
Physiological: Basic Care and
   Comfort

28-7. Which of the following is a nonpharmacological intervention to relieve afterpains? Have the client

a. lie prone with a small pillow under her abdomen.

b. take a hot shower, running water over her breasts.

c. breastfeed her baby.

d. empty her bladder.

c
Comprehension
Planning
Promotion: Growth and
   Development

28-8. A woman gave birth to her second baby yesterday. She is getting ready to go home and is concerned that her older daughter may not accept the new baby. The nurse should suggest that

a. the older daughter come to the hospital to take the baby home.

b. another adult play with the older child when the mother is caring for the baby.

c. the father carry the new baby into the house so the mother's arms are free to hold the older children.

d. the parents give the older child more responsibility and assure her that she is now a big girl.

a

Knowledge

Planning

Physiological: Basic Care and
  Comfort

28-9. To reduce edema and numb perineal tissues, what is often used immediately after birth of the baby?

a. ice pack

b. heat lamp

c. topical anesthetic

d. antibiotic ointment

b

Application

Implementation

Physiological: Reduction of
  Risk Potential

28-10. A woman has just had her first baby by cesarean birth. This is her first postoperative day. She asks the nurse why she has to turn, cough, and deep breathe when it causes her incision to hurt so much. The nurse should tell her that

a. she needs to blow off the anesthetic she received during surgery.

b. decreased mobility and lowered resistance put her at risk for lung infection, and the exercises will help prevent that.

c. the physician has ordered the exercises for her to help her recover faster.

d. the turning, breathing, and coughing will decrease the amount of pain medication she requires.

a

Application

Implementation

Physiological: Reduction of
  Risk Potential

28-11. A woman has given birth to her first baby by cesarean birth. This is her first postoperative day. She asks the nurse why she should not drink colas, use a straw, or eat sweets. The nurse should tell her that

a. these practices tend to increase gas for some mothers.

b. since she is nursing, these practices are not good for her baby.

c. her intestines will be sluggish for a few days and absorption will be decreased.

d. these restrictions are necessary to prevent nausea.

d

Comprehension

Planning

Physiological: Basic Care and
  Comfort

28-12. A 24-year-old gravida 2 has had a cesarean birth. During the first day or two, which of the following nursing interventions will improve her intestinal motility?

a. Encourage leg exercises at least every 2 hours.

b. Help her turn, cough, and deep breathe every 2 hours.

c. Provide analgesics (as ordered) to minimize pain.

d. Have her ambulate in her room.

b
Comprehension
Implementation
Physiological: Basic Care and
    Comfort

28-13. A woman has had a cesarean birth. After assessing her complaint of pains in her abdomen, the nurse believes that the client is experiencing gas pains. Which of the following nursing actions will help to minimize the client's gas pains?

a. Avoid serving protein or solid foods for the first 48 hours after the cesarean.

b. Avoid giving the client carbonated drinks or a straw with other fluids.

c. Give the client a hot drink several times a day.

d. Position the client in a semi-Fowler's position.

a
Comprehension
Planning
Promotion: Growth and
    Development

28-14. In order to provide an environment that is most conducive to bonding, the most important action by the nurse would be to provide

a. a secure environment and time for the family to be together during the first hour after birth.

b. a home-like environment with all of the medical equipment hidden from view.

c. adequate time following birth for the mother to rest before having her care for the baby.

d. time for the mother and father to be alone together before interacting with the baby.

d
Comprehension
Evaluation
Promotion: Growth and
    Development

28-15. Which of the following examples of charting would objectively indicate that the mother has bonded with the infant?

a. gave return bath demonstration

b. nursed the baby without difficulty

c. stated that she loves the baby

d. cuddled and called the baby by name

a
Application
Planning
Physiological:
    Pharmacological and
    Parenteral

28-16. One hour after birth of her baby, a woman was given methylergonovine maleate (Methergine) 0.2 mg IM. This medication was given to accomplish which goal? To

a. control uterine bleeding

b. prevent breast engorgement

c. relieve episiotomy pain

d. lower blood pressure

b
Comprehension
Planning
Promotion: Growth and
    Development

28-17. A woman gave birth to her second baby yesterday. She asks the nurse when she and her husband can resume sexual intercourse. The nurse should encourage the couple to wait until

a. after the woman has had her 6-week check-up.

b. the client's episiotomy has healed and the lochia has stopped.

c. the lochia is no longer red and the client's vagina is nontender.

d. after the client's first menstrual period.

b
Application
Analysis/Diagnosis
Promotion: Growth and
    Development

28-18. A client gave vaginal birth to her first baby 10 hours ago. She is fidgeting and states her bottom feels like it is tight and on fire. Her vital signs are stable. Her baby did not breastfeed well at the last feeding, and she says she really doesn't know much about infant care and feeding. At this time, which of the following problems has priority for this client?

a. knowledge deficit

b. pain

c. ineffective breastfeeding

d. altered parenting

a
Comprehension
Assessment
Promotion: Growth and
    Development

28-19. On her first postpartal day a client talks repeatedly about her labor and delivery experiences. This activity is important for her to

a. integrate and come to terms with her experiences.

b. keep from becoming socially isolated.

c. develop attachment and maternal role behaviors.

d. adjust to the loss of her independence.

d
Application
Analysis/Diagnosis
Promotion: Growth and
    Development

28-20. A 15-year-old client has just delivered her first child vaginally. She had no prenatal care and her knowledge about caring for herself and her baby is limited. Which of the following nursing diagnoses would have priority for this client?

a. risk for fluid volume deficit

b. altered nutrition less than body requirements

c. risk for urinary retention

d. knowledge deficit

a

Application

Implementation

Physiological: Reduction of
Risk Potential

28-21. A woman is 4 days postpartum and breastfeeding her baby. She tells the office nurse that she does not feel well and that her lochia is still bright red. The nurse should tell her to

a. come into the office to see the physician about her symptoms.

b. decrease her activity and increase her fluid intake.

c. massage her uterus and increase the frequency of her Kegel exercises.

d. take her temperature and call the doctor only if she has a fever.

c

Comprehension

Planning

Promotion: Prevention and
Early Detection

28-22. Discharge teaching should include teaching the woman to contact her caregiver right away if she develops

a. thin, pink vaginal discharge during the first postpartal week.

b. uncomfortable breast engorgement.

c. calf pain or redness.

d. episiotomy or hemorrhoid pain.

b

Comprehension

Implementation

Promotion: Growth and
Development

28-23. Which of the following methods would be most effective in teaching parents how to bathe their baby?

a. Explain how to do it, then answer their questions.

b. Show them how to bathe the baby, then watch while they do it.

c. Provide a videotaped demonstration so they can watch it as many times as they like.

d. Explain how to bathe the baby and give them written instructions to take home with them.

b

Application

Assessment

Physiological:
Pharmacological and
Parenteral

28-24. One hour after birth of her baby, a woman has been given methylergonovine maleate (Methergine) 0.2 mg IM. To evaluate for *side effects*, the nurse should

a. palpate the client's uterus.

b. check the client's blood pressure.

c. keep an intake and output record.

d. auscultate the client's lung sounds.

a

Application

Assessment

Promotion: Prevention and
Early Detection

28-25. Which of the following women is a candidate for receiving rubella vaccine in the postpartal period? One

a. whose rubella titer is less than 1:10

b. whose rubella titer is more than 1:10

c. who is Rh negative with an Rh positive baby

d. who is ELISA antibody-positive

Chapter 29
Home Care of the Postpartal Family

b
Application
Analysis/Diagnosis
Promotion: Growth and
    Development

1. A baby is was born at 8 p.m. yesterday, at 40 weeks gestation, average weight for gestational age. He is now 24 hours old. At 4:00 p.m. his vital signs were axillary temp-98.2, apical pulse-180/min, respirations-40/min. Now (at 8:00 p.m.) his vital signs are ax.temp-97.8, apical pulse-130/min, respirations-30/min. Circumcision was performed at noon today; there has been no excessive bleeding. He has passed 1 stool and voided once since birth. Do these data meet the minimal criteria for discharge of newborns?

   a. No, because of the respiratory rate.

   b. No, because of the apical pulse data.

   c. No, because of the voiding data.

   d. No, because of the temperature.

d
Application
Assessment
Promotion: Growth and
    Development

29-2. A baby boy is 24 hours old. He was born at 39 weeks' gestation and average weight for gestational age. His vital signs are within normal limits and have been stable for the past 18 hours. He has passed meconium stool and has urinated 3 times since birth. He has not been circumcised. He has breastfed satisfactorily every 3 hours since birth; he has no jaundice. What other information does the nurse need in order to meet the minimal criteria for discharge of this infant?

   a. Has the mother received a RhoGAM injection?

   b. What is the baby's length and weight?

   c. How many siblings does he have at home?

   d. Was his first hepatitis B vaccine administered or scheduled?

b
Knowledge
Planning
Promotion: Growth and
    Development

29-3. In which sleep-wake state is there rapid eye movement (REM)?

   a. deep sleep

   b. light sleep

   c. drowsy

   d. crying

c

Application

Planning

Physiological: Reduction of
Risk Potential

29-4. The nurse makes a home health visit on day 5 postpartum. The client says that she "wets her pants" when she laughs or coughs. In addition to referring her to the health care provider, an appropriate nursing intervention would be to

a. obtain a clean-catch urine specimen.

b. take the client's temperature.

c. teach muscle tightening exercises (Kegels).

d. advise her to limit her fluid intake.

a

Application

Planning

Physiological: Reduction of
Risk Potential

29-5. A client is 6 weeks postpartum. She has been taking supplemental iron. Her hemoglobin is 8 g/dl and hematocrit is 32 percent. What action should the nurse take?

a. Refer her to the physician/midwife.

b. Advise her to increase her iron dosage.

c. Do nothing-these are acceptable values.

d. Assess her knowledge of iron-rich foods.

b

Knowledge

Assessment

Safety: Management of Care

29-6. Which of the following has created the trend toward shorter hospital stays after delivery?

a. research that validates the safety of short stays

b. efforts to contain health care costs

c. cooperative efforts between caregivers and families

d. the need to improve access to quality care

c

Knowledge

Planning

Physiological: Reduction of
Risk Potential

29-7. The American Academy of Pediatrics (AAP) Committee on Fetus and Newborn has developed minimum criteria to guide the timing of early discharge to enhance excellence in maternal-newborn care. Minimal criteria for the discharge of newborns include

a. The newborn's vital signs within normal limits and have been stable for 8 hours preceding discharge.

b. The newborn has urinated at least once and has active bowel sounds.

c. There has been no significant jaundice in the first 24 hours of life and newborn screening tests have been completed.

d. At least one feeding has been successfully completed and the baby's ability to suck and swallow has been observed.

a
Application
Analysis/Diagnosis
Safety: Management of Care

29-8. How are postpartal home visits *different* from community health visits? Home health visits are

a. more specifically focused than community health visits, and do not include long-term follow-up.

b. more comprehensive than community health visits, and include less physical assessment.

c. done for normal postpartal care, whereas community health visits are planned for sick patients.

d. for the purpose of preventing complications, whereas community health visits are for the purpose of early detection of complications.

d
Application
Implementation
Safety: Safety and Infection
    Control

29-9. A nurse is about to knock on the door of a home, when she hears shouting, a woman's screams, a baby crying, and several loud crashes. The nurse should

a. ring the doorbell and wait to see if someone comes to the door.

b. try the door, and if it is open go inside to try to protect the baby.

c. knock on the door and shout, "It's the nurse. Can I help you?"

d. return to the car, lock the doors, call 911 and the home care agency.

b
Knowledge
Assessment
Promotion: Growth and
    Development

29-10. Which of the following infant holds is best for burping the baby?

a. cradle hold

b. upright position

c. football hold

d. sling hold

d
Knowledge
Implementation
Promotion: Growth and
    Development

29-11. Which newborn position is best for drainage of mucous and allowing air to circulate around the cord?

a. prone

b. supine, head of bed elevated

c. supine, head of bed flat

d. side-lying with a rolled diaper behind the back

b
Knowledge
Assessment
Promotion: Growth and
    Development

29-12. Why should the newborn's position be changed periodically during the first few months of life? To prevent

a. sudden infant death syndrome.

b. permanently flattened areas of the skull.

c. aspiration of feedings.

d. gastroesophageal reflux.

a

Application

Implementation

Physiological: Basic Care and
    Comfort

29-13. The home health nurse arrives to find a mother bathing her 4-day-old infant in the kitchen. The baby is on a towel on the counter-top beside the sink; the bath water is in the sink. What should the nurse do?

a. observe and chat while the mother finishes the baby's bath

b. explain that the baby should not be bathed in a sink that is used to prepare food or wash dishes

c. show the mother how she can sit the baby in the water in the sink, supporting the back while bathing

d. finish the bath for the mother so she can put her feet up and rest while she watches you

d

Comprehension

Planning

Physiological: Basic Care and
    Comfort

29-14. Which of the following is a CORRECT step in cleaning a baby's eyes?

a. Use a moistened cotton-tip applicator, one end for each eye.

b. Wipe gently from outer to inner corner.

c. Use a dry cotton ball, one side for the right eye and then turn it over for the left eye.

d. Wrap a clean, damp washcloth around the index finger and use a different portion for each eye.

d

Application

Implementation

Promotion: Prevention and
    Early Detection

29-15. The nurse realizes that baby powder is not recommended any longer. However, a mother simply insists upon using it on her baby. Which response by the nurse would minimize the risk of harm to the baby?

a. "Sprinkle the powder in the dry diaper and then place the diaper on her."

b. "Apply the powder to her body when she is still slightly moist from her bath."

c. "Apply a thin film of baby oil before lightly dusting her with a talc-free powder."

d. "Shake talc-free powder onto your hands first and then apply it to her body."

a

Application

Analysis/Diagnosis

Promotion: Growth and
    Development

29-16. The mother of a week-old baby calls to say that for the past few days her baby has had 6 to 10 small, semiliquid, yellow stools per day. She is breastfeeding the baby exclusively. The nurse should advise her that

a. this is a normal stool pattern that will probably continue for a month or more.

b. until the stools are more formed, she should watch the baby for dry skin and other signs of dehydration.

c. to add a little formula to make a very thin rice cereal to give the baby once a day.

d. this stool pattern is most often seen in formula-fed babies, but it is nothing to worry about.

c

Application

Implementation

Safety: Safety and Infection
    Control

29-17. A home health nurse notices that there are several stuffed animals in the crib where the baby is sleeping. The nurse should

a. give positive reinforcement to the mother for providing developmental stimuli for her baby.

b. explain that stuffed animals collect dust and can aggravate allergic tendencies.

c. teach the mother that pillows and stuffed toys could cause a sleeping baby to suffocate.

d. remove the animals from the bed quietly, and not make a scene in front of the parents.

b

Knowledge

Assessment

Promotion: Growth and
    Development

29-18. The nurse should teach the parents to bathe their newborn

a. every day.

b. 2-4 times a week.

c. once a week.

d. twice a day.

b

Knowledge

Planning

Promotion: Growth and
    Development

29-19. Which infant sleep-wake state is the best for interacting with and receiving feedback from an infant?

a. drowsy

b. quiet alert

c. active alert

d. crying

c

Application

Planning

Safety: Management of Care

29-20. The home health nurse is making a previsit contact by telephone. It is important in this conversation for the nurse to

a. remind the mother to feed the baby just before the visit.

b. find out if the family has a bathtub or a shower.

c. clearly identify the purpose and goals of the visit.

d. do the interview part of the assessment ahead of time.

c

Application

Planning

Physiological: Reduction of
    Risk Potential

29-21. A mother calls to say that her baby's umbilical cord fell off 4 days ago, but that it is still moist and oozing. What should the nurse advise?

a. Clean the area 4 times a day with a cotton swab dipped in alcohol.

b. Clean the area 2 times a day with a cotton ball and hydrogen peroxide.

c. Make an appointment to see the baby's physician.

d. Observe it and call again in 3 days if it is not dry by then.

b
Application
Analysis/Diagnosis
Promotion: Growth and
    Development

29-22. A baby is 24 hours old. He was born at 39 weeks' gestation and average weight for gestational age. His respirations are 50/minute; they were 80/minute 4 hours ago. He has passed meconium stool and has urinated 3 times since birth. He has not been circumcised. He has breastfed every 3 hours since birth; he has no jaundice. Do these data meet the minimal criteria for discharge of newborns?

a. Yes, because all data are within normal limits.

b. No, because of the respiratory data.

c. No, because of the circumcision data.

d. Yes, *if* suck, swallow, and breathing were coordinated at feedings.

a
Comprehension
Assessment
Safety: Management of Care

29-23. For some mothers, short stays after birth can create problems. One reason for this is that

a. the mother's physical and psychological condition is not conducive to learning during the first 24 hours after birth.

b. there are no accepted criteria to use to evaluate whether the mother and baby are actually ready for discharge in 24 hours.

c. third-party payers (e.g., insurance companies) will not pay for complications that develop if a woman is discharged before 48 hours.

d. women who are discharged early feel they have less control over self- and infant-care decisions.

c
Application
Assessment
Safety: Management of Care

29-24. How is home care for the postpartal family *different from* nursing care in the hospital? In the home, the nurse

a. has more control over the environment for care.

b. teaches self- and infant-care techniques.

c. can interact with the family in a more relaxed setting.

d. assesses the physical condition of the mother and baby.

Chapter 30
The Postpartal Family at Risk

d
Application
Implementation
Physiological: Physiological
    Adaptation

1. A woman is 4 hours postpartum after a vaginal birth. She has had heavy vaginal bleeding since that time. Her bladder is not palpable, and her fundus is firm at 1 fingerbreadth below the umbilicus. The nurse should

   a. speed up the intravenous Pitocin.

   b. massage the client's fundus until the bleeding stops.

   c. assist the client up to the bathroom to void.

   d. notify the physician/midwife of her findings.

c
Application
Analysis/Diagnosis
Physiological: Physiological
    Adaptation

30-2. A woman is 4 hours postpartum after a vaginal birth. She has had heavy vaginal bleeding since that time. Her bladder is not palpable, and her fundus is firm at 1 fingerbreadth below the umbilicus. The nurse should suspect

   a. pelvic hematoma.

   b. uterine atony.

   c. genital tract lacerations.

   d. urine retention.

a
Comprehension
Planning
Promotion: Prevention and
    Early Detection

30-3. One of the most important measures for preventing mastitis in the breastfeeding mother is

   a. meticulous hand washing by the mother.

   b. limiting the baby's sucking to not more than 10 minutes on a breast.

   c. prophylactic antibiotics.

   d. washing the breasts with soapy water and rinsing well before and after feedings.

c
Application
Assessment
Physiological: Physiological
    Adaptation

30-4. A client has had pelvic cellulitis and a pelvic abscess for several days. She has not responded well to treatment. Therefore, the nurse should be alert for signs and symptoms such as

   a. uterine atony and increased bleeding.

   b. pain and redness in the calf of the legs.

   c. high fever, severe pain and abdominal distention.

   d. elevated blood pressure and retention of urine.

c
Comprehension
Planning
Physiological: Physiological
   Adaptation

30-5. A client has had pelvic cellulitis and a pelvic abscess for several days. She has not responded well to antibiotic therapy and still has a firm mass behind her cervix. The nurse should anticipate

a. an increase in the antibiotic dosage.

b. that she will need to discontinue the intravenous line and put in a saline lock.

c. that the abscess will need to be drained.

d. moving the woman to a medical-surgical unit.

a
Knowledge
Assessment
Physiological: Physiological
   Adaptation

30-6. The most common puerperal infection is

a. endometritis.

b. salpingitis.

c. pelvic cellulitis.

d. peritonitis.

d
Knowledge
Analysis
Physiological: Reduction of
   Risk Potential

30-7. Which of the following is a symptom of superficial thrombophlebitis?

a. positive Homan's sign

b. pain in the entire lower affected leg and foot

c. edema of the ankle and lower leg

d. tenderness over a portion of the vein and local redness

d
Application
Assessment
Psychosocial: Coping and
   Adaptation

30-8. A couple gave birth to their third child 2 days ago. In order to help determine if the mother is at risk for psychological maladjustment, the nurse should ask her

a. her age at the time her first baby was born.

b. if she feels confident in caring for the baby.

c. about the family income and fixed expenses.

d. how she reacted to the birth of her other children.

a
Comprehension
Planning
Psychosocial: Coping and
   Adaptation

30-9. A couple gave birth to their third child 2 days ago. The woman is diagnosed as suffering from depression. Prior to discharge the nurse should

a. refer the couple to a public health nurse.

b. arrange for short-term hospitalization in a private psychiatric facility.

c. develop an exercise program for her so she cannot sit around and become more depressed.

d. notify the community children's protective services to evaluate the home environment.

a

Comprehension

Planning

Promotion: Prevention and
    Early Detection

30-10. To help prevent postpartal thrombophlebitis after a cesarean
birth, the nurse should

a. encourage early ambulation.

b. provide increased fluids to enhance circulation.

c. massage the client's legs b.id. .

d. impose strict bed rest for the first 48 hours after delivery.

b

Comprehension

Assessment

Promotion: Growth and
    Development

30-11. A woman has just given birth to a 10-pound baby girl.
Midforceps were used and the estimated blood loss was 300
ml. At birth the placenta and membranes were carefully
inspected to determine

a. which side of the placenta was expelled first.

b. if they were expelled intact.

c. the age and size of the placenta.

d. the number of veins and arteries.

c

Application

Analysis/Diagnosis

Physiological: Reduction of
    Risk Potential

30-12. A woman has just given birth to a 10-pound baby girl.
Midforceps were used and the estimated blood loss was 300
ml. Since the birth, the woman has had a large amount of
lochia. Which of the following diagnoses would have priority
for her now?

a. possible retention of placental fragments

b. risk for altered parenting

c. risk for fluid volume deficit

d. urinary retention

d

Application

Planning

Physiological: Physiological
    Adaptation

30-13. Shortly after the birth of a 9-pound infant, the nurse finds that
the mothers lochia flow is heavy and her uterus is boggy. The
nurse should first

a. notify the obstetrician or midwife.

b. speed up the IV Pitocin.

c. help the client ambulate.

d. massage the fundus until it is firm.

c

Application

Planning

Physiological: Physiological
    Adaptation

30-14. After giving birth to a 9-pound infant by midforceps delivery,
a woman continued to have large amounts of lochia. Her
obstetrician performed bimanual uterine compression and the
lochia has decreased. In order to provide safety for the client,
the nurse should

a. massage her fundus every 15 minutes.

b. take her vital signs every 30 minutes.

c. check her lochia and uterine tone every 15 minutes.

d. have her contract and relax her perineum every 30 minutes.

a

Application

Implementation

Psychological: Physiological
    Adaptation

30-15. A woman has experienced an early postpartum hemorrhage. Her medical orders are oxygen per face mask at 6 to 8 L/min, vital signs every 15 minutes, and IV Pitocin (oxytocin). She complains that she is really tired and has no energy. The nurse should tell her that

a. the fatigue is a result of her blood loss.

b. she will slowly regain her energy in the next 2 weeks.

c. all postpartum clients are tired after labor and delivery.

d. she will feel better after a good night's sleep.

a

Application

Analysis/Diagnosis
    Physiological: Reduction
    of Risk Potential

30-16. Which of the following will provide the *earliest* symptom of postpartum hemorrhage?

a. large amount of blood on the pads and bed linen

b. drop in the client's blood pressure

c. increase in the client's pulse

d. decrease in urine output

c

Comprehension

Planning

Physiological: Reduction of
    Risk Potential

30-17. Which of the following can help prevent vulvar or vaginal hematoma?

a. having the client do Kegel exercises during pregnancy

b. elevating the client's hips and legs after the birth and keeping her in bed for at least 2 hours

c. applying an ice pack to the client's perineum during the first hour after birth and intermittently for the next 8 hours

d. helping the client to a sitz bath after the birth, as soon as she can walk

a

Application

Planning

Physiological: Reduction of
    Risk Potential

30-18. A 16-year-old client has given birth to her first child. The nurse carefully explains perineal care to her. The client's understanding and follow-through of perineal care are important *primarily to*

a. decrease the possibility of infection.

b. increase the client's comfort.

c. speed healing of her perineum.

d. help shrink the hemorrhoids.

c

Knowledge

Assessment

Promotion: Prevention and
    Early Detection

30-19. At the time of birth, the vagina and uterus of most women

a. are sterile.

b. contain no pathogens.

c. have pathogenic organisms that are capable of causing infection.

d. are infected if the membranes have been ruptured more than 24 hours.

c

Comprehension

Analysis

Physiological: Reduction of
Risk Potential

30-20. Which of the following clients is at high risk for postpartum uterine infection? One who

a. has given birth to a 6-pound, premature baby.

b. gave birth vaginally after 1 hour of pushing.

c. gave birth by cesarean section.

d. had rupture of membranes 4 hours before birth.

b

Application

Planning

Physiological: Reduction of
Risk Potential

30-21. A couple have had a baby by cesarean birth. When the nurse changes the dressing on the client's incision, the skin edges of the incision are red, edematous, and tender to the touch. The nurse's best intervention would be to

a. cleanse the wound with hydrogen peroxide.

b. chart observations and notify the physician.

c. chart observation of the first phase of the normal healing process.

d. observe the incision closely for the next 24 to 48 hours.

a

Knowledge

Assessment

Physiological: Reduction of
Risk Potential

30-22. When inspecting a woman's perineum for infection, the nurse uses the REEDA scale. The R stands for

a. redness.

b. rubra.

c. risk factors.

d. rugae.

c

Application

Implementation

Physiological: Physiological
Adaptation

30-23. A woman had a cesarean birth. The skin edges of her incision are red, edematous, and tender to the touch. The physician later removes the sutures from the abdominal incision and the wound gapes open. The client asks the nurse, "Why did the doctor take out my stitches? Obviously I am not healed yet." The nurse's best reply would be,

a. "The stitches had to be removed because they were infected."

b. "Your doctor will replace the stitches with stronger, hypoallergenic ones."

c. "Removing the stitches will allow the infected incision to drain."

d. "This will allow the infected incision to heal from the inside out."

a

Comprehension

Planning

Psychosocial: Coping and
    Adaptation

30-24. A client's cesarean incision has become infected. She is septic and has been placed in isolation in an intensive care unit. Since the baby can no longer room in, which of the following interventions would best promote bonding between the client and her infant?

a. Provide a picture of the baby for her.

b. Have the partner visit the baby more often.

c. Assure the client that she will be in isolation only a short time.

d. Listen while she goes over the details of the birth as often as she needs to.

b

Comprehension

Planning

Physiological: Physiological
    Adaptation

30-25. A couple has had their third baby by cesarean birth. The woman's incision has become infected and she has been placed in isolation. Since she cannot breast-feed her baby while she is in isolation, she must pump her breasts. The *most* important reason for pumping her breasts is to

a. prevent engorgement.

b. assure continued milk production.

c. remove the infected milk.

d. promote uterine involution.

b

Comprehension

Assessment

Physiological: Reduction of
    Risk Potential

30-26. A 19-year-old obese woman has just had her first baby by cesarean birth. She is bottle-feeding the baby. In addition to having had varicose veins during pregnancy, which of the following maternal factors also predisposes her to thrombophlebitis?

a. primigravida status

b. obesity

c. use of a lactation suppressant

d. young age

a

Comprehension

Planning

Physiological: Reduction of
    Risk Potential

30-27. A woman in labor has a history of varicose veins and several other factors that put her at high risk for thrombophlebitis. Which of the following nursing actions during labor would help to prevent thrombophlebitis?

a. Be sure she is well hydrated.

b. Insert an indwelling catheter to prevent bladder distention.

c. Position the client on her left side.

d. Maintain the client on bedrest.

b

Comprehension

Assessment

Physiological: Reduction of
    Risk Potential

30-28. A woman in labor has thrombophlebitis. During the intra- and postpartum periods, the nurses should be especially alert for signs of

a. fetal distress.

b. pulmonary embolism.

c. fluid overload.

d. hypertension.

d

Comprehension

Planning

Physiological:
    Pharmacological and
    Parenteral

30-29. After experiencing thrombophlebitis, a client is being discharged on warfarin (Coumadin). Discharge teaching should include which of the following safety instructions regarding this medication? Teach the client to

a. avoid walking long distances and climbing stairs.

b. avoid any lacerations, punctures, or bruising-type injuries.

c. keep an injectable form of warfarin available.

d. avoid taking aspirin and certain anti-inflammatory drugs.

c

Application

Analysis/Diagnosis

Physiological: Reduction of
    Risk Potential

30-30. A woman gave birth to an 8-pound baby girl 30 minutes ago. During the initial postpartal assessment, the nurse will assess her bladder. Which of the following observations would indicate that the nurse should be concerned about urinary retention?

a. complaint of pain in the lower back

b. voiding measured at 200 ml

c. palpable mass (distention) above the symphysis pubis

d. the client's complaint of discomfort while voiding

d

Knowledge

Analysis/Diagnosis

Physiological: Reduction of
    Risk Potential

30-31. Which of the following women is at high risk for uterine atony after birth? One who has had

a. an epidural anesthetic.

b. forceps-assisted birth.

c. precipitous childbirth.

d. prolonged labor.

c

Application

Evaluation

Physiological: Basic Care

30-32. A woman has experienced an early postpartum hemorrhage. Her medical orders are oxygen per face mask at 6 to 8 L/min., vital signs every 15 minutes, and IV Pitocin (oxytocin). In order to assess whether the fluid volume replacement is adequate for this client, the nurse must

a. write a nursing order to weigh the client daily.

b. assess her skin turgor for signs of dehydration.

c. assess hourly urine output.

d. regulate the IV to run at 125 ml/hour.

d
Application
Implementation
Physiological: Physiological
    Adaptation

30-33. A woman gave birth to her first baby vaginally with no problems, and was discharged from the birthing unit on the same day. The next day, the home health nurse finds a swelling of about 3 cm x 3 cm on the client's perineum. The woman says it has not changed in size during the last 12 hours and is a little tender. The nurse should tell the woman to

a. apply a warm compress to the area and call if the swelling does not resolve in 4 or 5 days.

b. call now to make an appointment to see the physician within the next 24-36 hours.

c. insert an indwelling catheter and accompany the client to the physician's office or emergency room.

d. apply an ice pack to the area and call if the swelling gets larger or does not resolve in 4 or 5 days.

b
Application
Implementation
Physiological: Reduction of
    Risk Potential

30-34. Several hours after giving birth, a client has a distended bladder and is unable to void. The nurse inserts a catheter and removes 1000 ml of urine from the client's bladder. What should the nurse do at this time?

a. Remove the catheter and encourage the client to void any remaining urine in the bladder.
b. Clamp the catheter for 1 hour and tape it to the client's leg.
c. Continue to drain urine from the bladder until the bladder is empty.
d. Remove the catheter and instruct the client in Kegel exercises to strengthen bladder contractions.